Calling the World to Christ

Calling the World to Christ

Luis Palau

Vance Christie

CF4KIDS

Published by
Christian Focus Publications, Geanies House, Fearn, Tain,
Ross-shire, IV20 1TW, Scotland, U.K.
www.christianfocus.com
Cover design by Daniel van Straaten
Cover illustration by Daniel van Straaten
Printed and bound in Denmark by Nørhaven

Primary source materials used in the writing of this book include: *Luis Palau: Calling America and the Nations to Christ*, by Luis Palau with David Sanford (Thomas Nelson Publishers, 1994); *The Impact of Luis Palau on Global Evangelism,* by Hongnak Koo (Credo House Publishers, 2010); *Palau: A Life on Fire*, by Luis Palau with Paul J. Pastor (Zondervan, 2019); The Luis Palau Association website (www.palau.org).

Contents

To our newest grandchild
Andi Noel
and to all Christian children.
May you know Jesus Christ
and make Him known to others.

A Christian Home and Church

Matilde Palau, a young Argentine woman, heard a knock at the front door of her home. Opening it, she found a tall, sharply dressed British gentleman standing on the step. He held a fine-looking book in one hand and a heavy walking stick, which was sometimes needed to ward off aggressive dogs, in the other.

'Buenos Dias, Senora,' he greeted Matilde pleasantly. Then holding up the book, he asked, 'Would you like a copy of the Word of God?'

Matilde was a devout Roman Catholic. She regularly attended Mass where she sometimes heard Scripture verses read. But it is not known whether she had ever owned a Bible of her own.

Gladly she received the attractive copy of the New Testament in Spanish, which was given to her free of charge. 'Muchos gracias,' she stated sincerely.

Matilde's life was very happy. She was married to her husband, Luis, who worked hard and provided well for them. They loved each other deeply and were joyfully anticipating the birth of their first child. However, for many years Matilde had been unable to find the spiritual peace that her soul craved. She faithfully attended Mass and confessed her sins to the priest. She served in church by playing the organ. She made promises to God and tried to keep them. Yet, something was missing. She did not have inner peace.

She immediately began to read the New Testament. So deep was her reverence for God's Word, that she read it on her knees! Soon she came to Matthew 5:8, where Christ Jesus stated: 'Blessed are the pure in heart, for they will see God.' Instead of being encouraged by Christ's words, she at first felt despair. 'That's it,' she thought, 'I will never see God. I know that I do not have a pure heart.'

As she was praying, however, the Lord spoke to her in her heart: 'My daughter, you are mine. You are forgiven.' She suddenly remembered John the Baptist's testimony about Jesus that she had often heard the priest quote at the Mass: 'Behold, the Lamb of God who takes away the sin of the world' (John 1:29).

Joy flooded her heart as she realized: 'This Lamb was for me! He came to take away my sin!' Her fears of 'I will never find peace with God and will never be forgiven' instantly vanished, as she trusted in Christ as the Lamb of God who had come to save her from her sins. At last she had found the spiritual peace and rest that her heart had longed to have for so many years.

Brimming over with joy, Matilde sought out the kindly British man who had given her the New Testament. His name was Edward Rogers. He had come to Argentina as a self-supporting missionary. During the week he worked as a high-ranking executive for the Shell Oil Company in Buenos Aires, the capital city of Argentina. On the weekend he carried out evangelistic work in Ingeniero Maschwitz (usually called simply Maschwitz), the small town where the Palaus lived, about thirty miles northwest of Buenos Aires. Mr. Rogers had also planted a Plymouth Brethren Chapel in Maschwitz, the first non-Catholic church in town.

After telling Mr. Rogers of her new-found peace from trusting in Jesus as her Savior, Matilde asked him, 'Should I leave the Catholic church?'

'No, no! Stay there,' he advised. 'Tell your friends what you've experienced. Tell them how the Lord has brought peace to your heart. Many of them are probably still searching for what you have found. Then, in the evenings, come join our Bible meetings in our little chapel.'

She did that for a time. Eventually she came to believe that her duty to the Catholic church was fulfilled, and she started attending the Brethren chapel services Sunday morning and evening.

Matilde desired her husband to have the same peace and joy that she had found. She tried to share with him about spiritual matters, but he made it clear he was not interested.

Though only in his early twenties, Luis was already enjoying considerable success as a businessman. He had his own construction company. In addition, he was a tough, muscular athlete who played soccer in his spare time. Though he was a member of the Catholic church, he viewed religion as a crutch to help the fearful and weak – something for women, children, and the elderly, but not for strong men like himself.

Luis drove his wife to church every Sunday. After dropping her off, he would go for a drink with his buddies then return when the service was over. But one Sunday evening he surprised Matilde by going into the chapel with her.

Right in the middle of the pastor's sermon, Mr. Palau suddenly stood up and announced: 'I receive Jesus Christ as my only and sufficient Savior.' Having made his simple, sincere declaration of faith in Christ, he then sat back down. From that night forward he was a totally devoted follower of Jesus.

Luis and Matilde's firstborn child was a son whom they named Luis Palau, Jr. He was born on November 27, 1934, a few months after his mother trusted in Christ and several months before his father became a Christian. In the decade that followed, five daughters were born to the couple.

When Luis and Matilde dedicated their young son to the Lord they prayed: 'Lord, here is Luisito. He is yours. Use him for your glory and as you wish, so many may come to know you through him.' They kept this prayer a secret just between them and God. So, their son did not know about their prayer for many years.

Later, when Luis entered his teen years, he was concerned about his future. 'My friends already know what they're going to do when they grow up,' he told his mother. 'I don't have a clue what I will do.'

She did not want to pressure her son with her own heart's desire that he would serve the Lord as a preacher of the gospel of salvation. So she wisely responded: 'You don't know what you will do, Luis, but God does. He will show it to you at the right time.'

Mr. and Mrs. Palau faithfully attended the Brethren church with their children. The tiny chapel measured only about 20 feet by 20 feet. Its walls and roof were made with sheets of corrugated metal. When the heavy winter rains poured down against the metal roof and walls, they nearly drowned out the sound of the congregation's singing and the voice of the preacher.

Young Luis gained many spiritual benefits from his years growing up in that small, humble church. In Sunday School he learned Bible stories and memory verses. The Lord's Supper was solemnly observed each Sunday morning. Mr. Rogers' clear preaching emphasized not only the problem of sin in each person's heart and life, but also God's gracious solutions of forgiveness, spiritual rebirth and eternal life through saving faith in Jesus. This helped prepare Luis's heart to believe in and receive Christ at a later time.

Luis's father enthusiastically assisted Mr. Rogers with evangelism and church planting in the surrounding area. Mr. Palau actively involved his family in those outreaches. Luis, his mother, and his sisters would ride with his father to nearby towns to hold street preaching meetings. The Palau children, seated on benches in the back of the truck, would throw out flyers, inviting people to a meeting to hear the gospel.

The family brought along a pump organ for Mrs. Palau to play at the meeting. This helped to draw people to listen to what was being shared. Mr. Rogers would preach, and Mr. Palau would tell his story of how he had become a Christian. His testimony always featured John 3:16: 'For God so loved the world, that he gave His one and only Son, that whoever believes in Him shall not perish but have eternal life.' That verse was always followed by Acts 16:31: 'Believe in the Lord Jesus, and you will be saved – you and your household.'

As Mr. Rogers and Mr. Palau spoke, Luis and his sisters would weave through the crowd, passing out gospel tracts. 'Have one of these!' Luis would offer, then add the suggestion, 'Go read it.' Some accepted their literature, while others teased or even insulted them.

Remarkably, over the course of several years, Mr. Rogers and Mr. Palau were used of the Lord to plant nine new churches around Buenos Aires. Every summer they selected a new town in which to minister. They would preach on the streets and gather new converts. Then as the year ended, they appointed leaders for a new church. Mr. Palau built each new church a simple chapel, complete with a baptistery and an outhouse. Around seventy-five years later, Luis would write: 'The nine churches they planted still exist today as a testament to their ministry.'

Boyhood Schooling and Sorrow

Luis went to the local public school until he was eight years old. He was an active, restless young boy with a rather independent spirit. Until his next oldest sister joined him a couple of years after he started attending, he was the only child of evangelical Christian parents in that school. Occasionally he was called names by fellow students and even by teachers. His teachers sometimes made him kneel on corn kernels in the corner of the schoolroom if he misbehaved. Once he was forced to do so because he refused to pray to the Virgin Mary.

In time, Luis's father decided to send him to Quilmes Preparatory School, a prestigious and disciplined private British boarding school near the capital of Buenos Aires. 'Luis,' Mr. Palau told his son, 'I want you to learn good English because it's the language of the future. I want you to receive the best possible education. One day I'd even like to send you to study at Cambridge University in England.'

Mr. Palau had been born in the Catalonia region of northeastern Spain and immigrated with his family to Argentina when around twelve years of age. Mrs. Palau was also the daughter of immigrants to Argentina. Her father was from Scotland and her mother was from France.

Luis and his sisters grew up speaking and reading both Spanish and English because their mother was bilingual. 'The boarding school at Quilmes will give you the opportunity to sharpen your English,' Luis's father encouraged him. 'It will be to your advantage to become completely bilingual, equally fluent in English and Spanish.' Neither Mr. Palau nor Luis had any way of foreseeing the huge part his becoming fully bilingual would play in his extraordinary future ministry career.

While at Quilmes, Luis greatly missed his parents and other family members. He was able to return home one weekend each month. His mother's parents lived only a couple of streets away from the boarding school, but the institution's strict rules did not allow him to visit or even phone them. However, he enjoyed his classes, sports, and other activities at the school.

In mid-December 1944, not long after his tenth birthday, Luis took his final exams at Quilmes and started preparing to return home for summer vacation.[1] When he unexpectedly received a phone call from his grandmother, contrary to school rules, he knew something must be wrong.

'Luis,' she informed him, 'your dad is very sick. We really have to pray for him. It's serious. Your mom wants you to come and see your dad.'

---

1 In that part of South America, well below the equator, the hot and cold seasons are the opposite of what they are in North America and Europe.

Although Luis's grandmother did not give him any other details, he had a terrible feeling that his father was dying. The next morning, December 17, his grandmother came and put him on a train bound for home. To Luis it seemed like the three-hour train trip would never end. He sat in silence, staring ahead but seeing nothing. He could not shake the dreadful feeling that his father had already died and that he would arrive home too late to say goodbye to him.

When Maschwitz was finally reached, Luis bounded off the train and ran through the town to his home. The intense summer heat did not slow him down. When he came within earshot of his house, he heard the traditional wailing that many Argentines carried out after the death of a family member. Some of his non-Christian aunts and uncles were moaning and crying. 'Why does God allow this?' they asked. 'So many little children left without a father. Oh! what will Matilde do?'

Brushing past his relatives, Luis burst into the house and ran straight to his dad's bedroom. The father's body was lying in bed, as if he were asleep, but he had died a few hours earlier. Luis was shocked at the appearance of his dad's body, which was discolored yellow, and dehydrated. He was even more stunned to realize that he would never again be able to talk, laugh, work or play with his beloved Papito. He hugged and kissed his father's body and wept bitterly at his unspeakable loss.

Luis's mother stepped behind him and put her hands on his shoulders. 'Luisito, Luisito,' she said softly, 'I must talk to you and tell you how it was.' Pulling him away from the bedside, she led him outside.

'When the doctors realized they weren't able to do anything else for your father, we decided to call you so you could hurry home. It was obvious he was dying. As we gathered around his bed, praying and trying to comfort him, he seemed to fall asleep. He was struggling to breathe, but suddenly he sat up and began to sing.'

Luis looked up at his mother, hardly believing what she was telling him. Referring to part of a song they sometimes sang at church, she continued: 'Papito began to sing:

"Bright crowns up there,
    bright crowns for you and me.
Then the palm of victory,
    the palm of victory."

'He sang it three times, all the while clapping in rhythm as you children did when you sang it in Sunday School. Then, when Papito could no longer hold up his head, he fell back the pillow and said, "I'm going to be with Jesus, which is far better" (Philippians 1:23).'

Luis later learned that his father had developed a cough that slowly took hold of his chest. Since he was young and strong, he was unconcerned about the cough, thinking he would easily beat it. But it deepened into pneumonia, and by the time he went to the hospital there was nothing the doctors could do for him. Due to World War II, which was taking place at that time, penicillin was in terribly short supply in Argentina. The doctors had no other powerful antibiotics with which to treat Luis's dad, and he needed to return home knowing he was dying. Though the family sent for Luis immediately, his father passed away before he could reach him. Mr. Palau was only thirty-four years old when he died.

After another year of schooling at Quilmes, Luis then transferred to St Alban's College, which was connected with the Church of England and the Cambridge University Overseas Program. St Alban's was an exclusive and expensive British school located in the rich suburbs south of Buenos Aires. Half the students at the private, all-boys school were sons of British railway, banking, shipping or lumber executives, while the other half were Argentine boys whose parents could afford to send them there.

Weekday mornings the classes that the Argentine government required were taught entirely in Spanish. In the afternoons the subjects that were part of the Cambridge Overseas Program were taught only in English. In this way, Luis came to speak, read and write both Spanish and English equally well. The St Alban's program was designed in such a way that by the time students graduated they had completed high school and the equivalent of two years of junior college, and were qualified for advanced studies at Cambridge University.

Life at St Alban's was highly disciplined. All the students wore school uniforms. Thirty boys shared a large dorm room, sleeping on beds that were lined up in neat rows. The students all got up at the same time, made their beds, cleaned their small living space, and neatly combed their hair 'just so.' Like the military, they stood in orderly lines and carried out marching drills.

The students played sports like cricket and rugby. They were not allowed to play Latin America's favorite sport of *futbol* (soccer) on campus because it was looked down upon as being for 'naps' (street people, the uneducated). Despite that, Luis and other daring classmates risked playing soccer behind a grove of trees on the edge of the schoolgrounds. Luis enjoyed playing sports as well as the pranks, jokes and traps the students would play on each other and their teachers.

Becoming a Christian

For several years Luis had been raised in a Bible-teaching church where he regularly heard the gospel clearly taught. He had learned many Bible stories and could quote numerous Scripture verses from memory. Now he was attending an Anglican school and had even been confirmed as a professing Christian by a Church of England bishop. However, in Luis's heart, he knew he was not a true Christian because he had never trusted in Christ as his Savior from sin.

One of the few strong, Bible-believing Christians at St Alban's was a teacher named Charles Cohen. Each February he led a two-week Christian camp in the mountains for dozens of boys during their summer vacation from school. In December 1946, not long after Luis turned twelve years of age, Mr. Cohen invited him to the camp and even offered to pay his way so he could attend.

Luis did not want to attend the camp because his school friends did not consider it a 'cool' thing to do. He knew a number of boys became Christians at the camp each year, and he thought he might be pressured to pray to receive Jesus as his Savior.

'I'm glad you will be going to the camp,' Luis's mother told him frankly, 'because I'm not sure you are a real, born-again Christian.'

'Oh, Mom, come on,' he protested, trying to pretend he was a true believer. But she knew he was not.

Luis had never been to camp before, and he gradually became excited about camping in the mountainous area of Azul in southern Argentina. At the camp he recognized most of the boys from St Alban's. There were fifty or sixty boys at the camp, and their counselors were from different British and American missionary organizations.

They used Argentine army tents, slept on foldable cots, and were taught how to rough it in the wild. They had a Bible teacher in the morning and another speaker at night. In addition to Bible lessons, they had Scripture memorization and singing every day. There was also plenty of time for old-fashioned British games like cricket and rounders.

Seven boys and a counselor stayed in each large army tent. During the second week of camp, after everyone had gone to bed, the counselor of each tent would take one boy per night out for a walk and one-on-one spiritual conversation. The main purpose of those conversations was to provide each boy with the opportunity to place his trust in Jesus as Savior. Or if a boy had already made a confession of faith in Christ, he could solidify his previous commitment and be provided with further assurance of his salvation from the Bible.

On the last night of camp, it was Luis's turn to have this talk with his counselor, Frank Chandler. When Frank came to get him for their walk outside, Luis pretended he was already asleep on his cot. Frank shook his shoulder, but Luis continued to act as if he were sound asleep. Frank knew he was faking, so turned over his cot and dumped him on the ground! 'Come on, Luis,' he said, 'get up.'

When they left the tent, the wind was picking up and it seemed like it would soon start to rain. A thunderstorm was coming their way. They walked to a fallen log not far from the tent and sat on it. Frank pulled out his flashlight, opened his New Testament, and got straight to business by asking, 'Luis, are you a born-again Christian or not?'

'I don't think so,' the boy responded.

'Well, it's not a matter of whether you think so or not. Are you or aren't you?'

'No, I'm not.'

'Luis,' Frank pressed further, 'if you were to die tonight, would you go to heaven or hell?'

The boy sat quietly a moment, a bit taken aback, then answered honestly, 'I'd go to hell.'

'Why?'

Luis immediately thought of several of his sins and shortcomings. 'Well, I have a foul attitude, a dirty mouth and a bad temper. I swear a lot when things don't go my way. And I'm not nice to my sisters.'

'Okay, then,' Frank stated, acknowledging the boy's confessions. Then he asked, 'But is hell where you want to go?'

'No!' Luis responded emphatically. 'I want to go to heaven.'

'Do you know what you need to do?'

'Yes – believe in the Lord Jesus Christ.'

'That's right,' the counselor affirmed. 'Let me read to you.' He turned to Romans 10:9-10 and read those verses. Luis had heard them countless times throughout his life, but that night they took on a new and personal meaning.

Frank read the verses again, this time inserting Luis's name into them: 'If you confess with your lips, Luis, that Jesus is Lord and believe in your heart, Luis, that God raised Him from the dead, then you, Luis, will be saved. For man believes with his heart and so is justified, and he confesses with his lips and so is saved.'

Frank then asked, 'Luis, do you believe in your heart that God raised Jesus from the dead?'

'Yes, I do.'

'Are you ready to confess Him as your Lord right now?'

'Yes.'

By that time the first big drops of the advancing summer storm had begun to fall. Despite that, Frank said, 'All right, let's pray.' He put his arm around the boy and led him in a prayer.

Luis prayed simply but sincerely: 'Lord Jesus, I believe You were raised from the dead. I confess You with my lips. Give me eternal life. I want to be Yours. Save me from hell. Amen.'

Frank and Luis ran through the rain back to the tent. As they entered it, Luis called out excitedly to the other boys, 'I've got eternal life! I've got eternal life!' He crawled under his blanket with his flashlight and wrote in his Bible: 'February 12, 1947 – I received Jesus Christ.'

When Luis returned to St Alban's he eagerly told his friends that he had become a Christian. The Anglican church services the students were required to attend each week became more meaningful to him. He also actively attended and helped out with the Crusaders youth group that met in Mr. Cohen's home on Sunday afternoons. Luis became a much better student in his school studies, especially in Mr. Cohen's Acts of the Apostles Bible class. He began to study his Bible every day. He also exchanged letters often with Frank Chandler, who encouraged him in his new Christian faith.

Trials and Temptations

For almost a year Luis was an 'excited, eager, happy Christian.' Then he experienced a series of trials and temptations that led to his losing his spiritual interest and enthusiasm. He knew he was still a Christian, but he grew distant from the Lord.

One Sunday while returning from a Crusaders youth group meeting, Luis accidentally (or 'carelessly' as he himself said) left his Bible on a streetcar and was unable to get it back. As a result, he stopped reading the Bible daily, became irregular in attending weekly Crusaders meetings, and lost his excitement for his Bible classes at school.

Another incident that contributed to Luis's sudden spiritual decline was a severe punishment he received from Mr. Cohen around that same time. Luis was then taking an art class and not doing well in it. One day he was showing off to some of his friends when Mr. Thompson, the new art teacher, walked over and made a rather sarcastic remark about Luis's poor painting of a tree.

As the instructor walked away, Luis responded with some foul word in Spanish which he supposed

Mr. Thompson, recently arrived from England, would not understand. The rest of the class understood Luis perfectly and laughed.

'What did you say, Palau?' the teacher asked.

'Oh, nothing, Mr. Thompson, sir,' Luis replied. 'Nothing, really.'

Twice more the instructor asked Luis to repeat the word, but he refused. 'All right!' Mr. Thompson then snapped. 'Go see the master on duty.'

Luis's jaw dropped in disbelief, and his classmates became silent. This was the ultimate punishment. When a student was sent to the master in charge of discipline for the day, the boy had to explain why he was there, then accept whatever punishment the master decided was appropriate. The teachers took turns serving as disciplinarians. Luis 'almost died inside' when he saw that Mr. Cohen was on discipline duty that day.

'Come in, Palau,' he directed. 'Why are you here?'

'Mr. Thompson sent me.'

'Is that so? Why?' To Luis, Mr. Cohen looked and sounded terribly cold toward him. Luis had spent a lot of time with Mr. Cohen and looked up to him as an older Christian. Now, however, the teacher seemed very distant.

'Well, I said a bad word,' the student confessed.

'Repeat it,' Mr. Cohen instructed. At first Luis refused, but when the master insisted, he finally complied.

For a few seconds Mr. Cohen did not move or say anything. Instead, he just sat there staring at Luis with an expression that showed he was obviously disappointed and perhaps even disgusted with him. At last, he reached for the flat wooden cricket bat that was used to administer corporal punishment to seriously disobedient students. 'You know, Palau, I'm going to give you six of the best.'

Luis could not believe his ears. That was the maximum number of swats given for any punishment!

To make matters worse, before paddling Luis, Mr. Cohen severely accused him of being a complete hypocrite. The instructor plainly stated some of the faults he had observed in Luis's attitudes and behavior and then concluded by stating: 'You come to Bible class all right, but you are a hypocrite.' Those words stung Luis more than the six swats which made it difficult for him to sit down in the days that followed.

Eventually Luis would conclude: 'What Mr. Cohen said and what he did were both medicine for me. But it took years before I realized it.'

At that time, Luis hated Mr. Cohen for months. He would not look at him or say hello to him. He stopped going to Crusaders meetings altogether and quit paying attention in Mr. Cohen's Bible classes. He went through the motions of going to church because students had to attend, but he was now totally disinterested in the services.

Luis started to 'stretch' and disobey some of the behavioral boundary lines that had been set for him by his school, his mother, and the church. At that time, he believed it was sinful to go to school dances or to read magazines about car racing and sports on Sunday. Yet he did those things anyway. He joined his old group of non-Christian friends, began 'talking rough' again, and developed an overall bad attitude toward life.

He felt worldly, sinful and guilty. During his final few years at St Alban's, he did not live for God at school or during his summers at home. Deep down inside he knew he still belonged to Christ. But he gave in to the pressure he and his unbelieving friends placed upon him not to be considered a fool by being an unashamed follower of Jesus.

An additional significant factor in Luis's spiritual decline during those years was the unresolved anger and bitterness he had over the painful financial difficulties his family experienced after his father's death. Mr. Palau was a highly successful businessman who had several commercial ventures. He also owned or was purchasing different properties as well as a lot of work equipment and supplies. However, when he died so suddenly and unexpectedly, he left no will providing for his family or paperwork that explained his many complicated business dealings.

Mrs. Palau knew nothing about her husband's business, so hired a man to manage it for their family. He instead cheated the Palaus out of their money and left the family very poor. In addition, immediately after Mr. Palau's death, a number of people began demanding money from the family company. Some took possession of work equipment or supplies, claiming they were their own rather than the Palaus'.

Luis was filled with rage toward the man who had mismanaged the business and left their family moneyless. Luis even wished he could destroy the man! He also blamed God for most of their troubles.

Knowing her husband's strong desire for Luis to be educated at St Alban's and Cambridge, Mrs. Palau did everything she could and made deep financial sacrifices to keep her son in school. Luis received financial assistance from a British charity to cover part of the cost of his education at St Alban's. For a few years he lived with his grandparents in Quilmes and commuted to school to save money.

At last the family's financial situation became so desperate that Luis's mother informed him he would not be able to take the final year at St Alban's which would have qualified him to attend Cambridge University. Luis's mom and sisters were going to move several hundred miles north to Cordoba. He would need to go to work to help support the family. He felt like all his plans and dreams for completing his education and becoming a wealthy businessman had been shattered.

While living in Quilmes, Luis attended the Brethren church there occasionally, but only to please his grandmother who had become a Christian. His new set of friends in Quilmes were not Christians. They liked to have a good time but did not get into trouble. They drank a little alcohol without getting drunk, went dancing, and attended soccer games on Sundays. Though Luis's conscience was not comfortable participating in some of those activities due to his conservative upbringing, he did so anyway because he did not want his friends to think he was weird.

Luis faced a personal moral crisis when Carnival Week arrived in 1952. He was then seventeen years old. Carnival Week in Latin America occurs the week before Lent and is followed by forty days of confession and penance leading up to Easter. During Carnival Week many people allow themselves to have 'a good time' without worrying about moral restraints. It was not unusual for young people to experience their first night of drunkenness or worse forms of immorality during Carnival Week.

At first the thought of joining his friends at Carnival Week seemed exciting to Luis. As the week drew closer, however, he started feeling convicted and even fearful over his own unspiritual condition. He knew that if he went to Carnival Week, temptation would overwhelm him, and he would be engulfed by sin. He feared God might abandon him to his sin if he entered into this all-out mockery of everything he had been taught while growing up.

'Toying with the world is one thing,' he thought, 'but abandoning self-respect and flaunting God's moral law is something altogether different. I want no part of it.'

To make matters worse, his grandparents were out of town that weekend and the house was empty. He was all on his own. The next day his friends would come to pick him up for the first day of the carnival festivities. 'There is no way I have the strength to simply tell them I'm not going,' he reflected. 'I have to have a reason not to go.'

Falling to his knees beside his bed, Luis pleaded and bargained with God: 'Get me out of this situation, and I will give up everything that's of the world. I will serve You and give my whole life to You. Just get me out of this!'

When Luis awoke the next morning, he sat up and yawned. His mouth felt strange. Touching it, he discovered it was extremely swollen. Stumbling to a mirror, he saw that his mouth looked like he had a ping-pong ball in it. When he tried to smile, it looked like he had just come home from the dentist. 'God has answered my prayer!' he exclaimed aloud.

He phoned one of his friends and told him, 'I can't go to the dance tonight, and I won't be going to the carnival at all this week.'

'Come on, Luis!' the friend protested. 'Everything has been planned.' When Luis would not change his mind, the friend stated, 'I'm coming over. You must be crazy.'

He arrived a few minutes later with three or four other guys and gals. 'The swelling will go down,' they tried to persuade him. 'You should change your mind.'

By then he had firmly made up his mind, and he resisted until they left. When he went back into the house, he tore up all his soccer and car-racing magazines and broke many of his record albums. He viewed them as having played a part in drawing his heart away from the Lord and to the temptations of the world. He had also taken up the habit of smoking tobacco with a pipe. He now broke his pipe, believing he should leave behind that practice as well.

The next day he went to church in the morning and evening. To him it seemed like the rest of the town was frolicking in sin, but he was glad to have escaped. He also bought himself a new Bible and started reading and studying it regularly.

That was an important turning point for Luis, spiritually and even emotionally. After that, he never again went back on his commitment to live for the Lord. Far from feeling oppressed by that commitment, he became excited about the future. 'Life perked up and had meaning again,' he afterward testified.

Learning to Trust God

Luis landed a job as a junior employee-in-training at the Bank of London in Buenos Aires. With his British education and bilingual abilities, he did well and was quickly promoted. After a period of time, he requested and was granted a transfer to the Bank of London in Cordoba. There he could be with and better support his mother and sisters.

The Palaus rented a small house in which they all lived. The house had a garage which served as the bedroom for Luis's sisters. Since he was the only brother, he slept in the tiny living room on a bed that doubled as a couch.

Luis worked full-time at the bank and received a modest salary. However, this could not begin to cover all the living expenses his family had. At one point they fell nine months behind on their rent. Their landlord patiently worked with them, until they were able to fully repay what they owed. The owner of the corner grocery store similarly extended them credit. Occasionally a little extra money would come in, and Mrs. Palau would go and pay people what they were owed.

On one memorable occasion, money was tighter than usual, and the Palaus expected, at last, to be thrown out of their house because they were several months behind on their rent. Just at that point of crisis, a letter was received from a past acquaintance who confessed:

'Mrs. Palau, I am embarrassed to tell this to you. Years ago, when you were in trouble, I lied to you. I took a tractor that I said was broken. In fact, it worked perfectly well. I have used it for years, and I'm ashamed that I did this to you – a widow with six children!'

The man signed the letter and included a check in the envelope for a substantial amount of money. He repaid her for the expensive tractor and added a considerable amount of interest he figured he owed. The Palaus were able to stay in their home, and their faith in God was greatly strengthened.

Because the Palaus were bilingual, people thought they were upper-class. And because Luis worked at a bank, they assumed the family was well-off. Actually, they were very poor.

Sometimes all they had for a meal was a cup of coffee and one loaf of French bread divided into seven parts. Once in a while Mrs. Palau would scrape together enough money to buy a steak, which was then cut into seven small portions, one for each family member. Regardless, they would always get on their knees and thank the Lord for their food.

Luis's mother never complained or expressed anger toward God over how difficult their family's life had become. She and her children trusted the Lord because they had no one else to trust. Mrs. Palau often reminded her children of various Bible verses she and they had memorized years earlier: 'Seek first God's kingdom and His righteousness, and all these things [material needs] will be given to you as well' (Matthew 6:33); 'Trust in the Lord with all your heart' (Proverbs 3:5a); 'My God shall supply all your need according to His riches in glory by Christ Jesus' (Philippians 4:19, KJV).

Mrs. Palau was able to earn a little money by translating books into Spanish for Christian ministries and by doing translation work for corporations. Eventually two of Luis's sisters also got work. After several years, the Palaus were at last able to say, 'We don't owe money to anyone.'

Throughout those years of tight finances, life for Luis and his family members revolved around work, education, and church activities. In addition to church meetings, they did all they could to help spread the gospel in Cordoba, a city of more than 750,000 inhabitants. They held children's outreach meetings in their home and in the open air, and actively participated in evangelistic street meetings.

Soon after arriving in Cordoba, Luis became fully involved in the Plymouth Brethren assembly there. George Mereshian, a full-time missionary who served with the church, saw great potential in this zealous young Christian. For the next three years Mr. Mereshian met with Luis for Bible study and Christian living training. They met three days per week and for three hours each session.

Luis did well in his work at the bank and was put in charge of superintending its overseas banking transactions. He found he could complete his daily work in a few hours. With full permission from his supervisors, he was permitted to devote the rest of his work time to his Bible studies! His bank co-workers began to call him 'Pastor'.

For some time Luis felt God was asking if he would be willing to do anything for Him. He wanted to say 'yes', but hesitated due to an unusual fear. He was afraid the Lord would ask him to be a missionary to lepers in Africa, where he would end up contracting that disease himself. He had been frightened by sermon illustrations about the dreaded disease and could not bear the thought of having it.

He sensed God was saying to him: 'It's either all or nothing. Are you willing to do *anything* for me?'

Kneeling by his bed one day, he finally committed himself: 'Yes, Lord, if it has to be, I'll even be a leper, for Your name's sake.'

While Luis would serve as a missionary for several years, he never became a leper. However, there were other deep personal and family sacrifices he would need to make in his service to Christ.

Luis joined George Mereshian and others from the church in going out to hold street preaching meetings. The first time Luis spoke publicly was at one of those meetings. He found that type of ministry exciting, challenging, rewarding, and enjoyable. Although initially he saw few people led to Christ through his street evangelism, he was learning the basics about how to effectively share the gospel with others.

Luis's first occasion to formally speak at church was at a Sunday afternoon youth meeting, which customarily was attended by adults as well. There was a crowd of 120 people, including Luis's proud, supportive relatives, and he was extremely nervous.

For weeks he had prepared for this occasion by studying Psalm 1 on his knees. He also studied the sermons of a prominent preacher of the past named Charles Spurgeon. Luis prayed and prayed for God to guide and use what he shared.

He prepared his notes well. He figured he had at least forty minutes of material to share and hoped he would not run past the time allotted for his presentation. When it came time to deliver the message, his throat was dry and the butterflies never stopped fluttering in his stomach. He practically read his notes word for word, and apparently 'raced' through them, for he finished the message in less than twelve minutes.

Afterwards he thought he had failed. Most of all, he was relieved it was over. From this humble first attempt at formal Bible teaching, Luis would go on to become a highly effective preacher of God's Word to millions of people throughout the world.

At 5 feet 7 inches tall, Luis was of average height for a South American man and possessed a medium build. He had dark brown, wavy hair, which he combed back from his forehead, and brown eyes. He had handsome facial features, which were made even more attractive by his ready smile.

Luis was personable and outgoing. He possessed a smooth facility of speech and was quick thinking on his feet. Spiritually, he had a hunger to learn the Scriptures, was strongly committed in his service of the Lord, and manifested a compelling desire to help lead non-Christians to Jesus the Savior.

By the time Luis was in his twenties, he and several other young men in the Brethren congregation held many evangelistic street meetings, sold Bibles, and handed out tracts. They also organized a Sunday school program, led youth meetings, visited the sick, held all-night prayer meetings, and developed a short daily radio program.

Active as they were in these commendable Christian ministries, Luis and the young men he was serving with still had spiritual struggles and discouragements. They especially needed to guard against pride and to work at keeping their thoughts clean, as many young people and not a few older Christians find they need to do.

Luis became frustrated that his evangelistic preaching seemed to have no spiritual power. He sought to be studied up, prayed up, and fired up in his ministries. Yet he saw no immediate fruit from his evangelistic efforts, except a few children who trusted in Christ as their Savior when he directed and taught Vacation Bible School.

Finally, he decided that if he did not see any converts by the end of the year, he would quit preaching. He would still be an active Christian and would continue to study the Bible and pray. But he would resign himself to simply assisting others in their ministries rather than leading in ministry himself.

'There's no use to my preaching,' he thought, 'if no one is coming to Christ.' When the end of the year came and went with no one turning to Jesus, Luis firmly concluded, 'I don't have the gift of evangelism.'

On a Saturday morning, just a few days into the new year, Luis sat down to read *The Secret of Happiness*, a book written by a famous young American evangelist named Billy Graham. Luis was blessed by Mr. Graham's thoughts on Christ's Beatitudes recorded in Matthew 5:3-12. Luis memorized the main points Graham made on each Beatitude.[1]

That evening Luis did not feel like going to the home Bible study he usually attended, but to support the church leaders he went anyway. When the intended speaker never arrived, Luis was asked to speak. 'Oh, I'm not prepared to speak tonight,' Luis tried to excuse himself. 'And besides, I forgot to bring my Bible.'

However, he was eventually persuaded. With just enough time to breathe a silent prayer, Luis urgently

---

1 Christ's teachings on how to live a life that is blessed by God.

asked the Lord for His help and blessing. He borrowed a New Testament, turned to Matthew 5, and read the first Beatitude. After repeating a few points he remembered from Billy Graham's book, he read the next verse and did the same.

When he came to verse 8, he read: 'Blessed are the pure in heart, for they will see God.' Suddenly a woman from the neighborhood stood and started to cry. 'Somebody help me!' she pleaded. 'My heart is not pure. How am I going to find God? Somebody tell me how I can get a pure heart.'

Luis directed her attention to 1 John 1:7 and read, 'The blood of Jesus, His Son, purifies us from all sin.' He went on to explain that Christ shed His blood on the cross so that those who trust in Him can be cleansed from sin and saved from its judgment. As a result, the woman believed in Jesus and went home that night with a pure heart that was at peace with God and overflowing with joy.

Through this incident Luis was reminded that it is God's Holy Spirit who convicts people of sin. God draws individuals to Jesus and salvation in His own good time. Luis returned home full of joy and praise to the Lord that He had used him in pointing this woman to the Savior.

Other people started coming to faith in Jesus through Luis's ministry. At first just a few, then more and more.

Called to Full-time Christian Ministry

Luis came to learn more about Billy Graham's large, successful evangelistic campaigns in major cities such as Los Angeles, Boston and London. 'Why can't we see this in our country?' Luis wondered. He began to dream that Argentina and eventually all Latin America could be reached on a large scale for Christ. 'Mass evangelism is the key!' he concluded.[1]

The more Luis read and prayed about mass evangelism, the more convinced he became it was the type of service the Lord wanted him to carry out. During this time, while in prayer, he began to envision himself reaching out to great crowds of people with the gospel. At first he wondered if this was just his imagination showing him he wanted to be a well-known preacher. But in the end he came to believe the Lord was laying on his heart what God was going to do.

If something like that were ever to come about, it would have to be the Lord's doing. Luis had none of the resources to accomplish anything like that. Without a miracle from God, he was helpless to bring it about.

---

1 Mass evangelism refers to efforts to preach the good news of salvation to very large numbers of people in a city or even a country.

For several years Luis shared with no one his dreams and desires about carrying out mass evangelism ministry. He continued to pray about the matter and to develop his abilities by actively preaching the gospel. His vision for mass evangelism never waned but, instead, continued to grow.

As people started realizing Luis's gift of evangelism, his speaking opportunities increased. His mother began urging him to leave the bank and devote himself to full-time ministry.

'But, Mom,' he pointed out, 'how are you going to live? We have a lot of mouths to feed.'

'Luis, you know if the Lord is in it, He will provide. He is no man's debtor.'

Once the two of them were walking out in the hills of Cordoba. Pointing to the horizon, Mrs. Palau stated: 'You have to get over there. You have to go preach. You need to go plant a church.'

Luis knew he ought to consider full-time ministry, but he had been putting it off. He had never felt the emotional pull of a call from God to go. So now he replied: 'But I don't feel the call. I don't have that final call that tells me it would be all right.'

'The call? What call?' she responded, then continued to press him: 'Christ gave the Great Commission 2,000 years ago, and you've read it all your life. How many times do you want Him to give the commandment before you obey it? It isn't a question of call; it's a question of obedience. The call He has given; it's the answer He's waiting for.'

Still Luis hesitated. He thought his mother was probably right, but he was not confident enough in the Lord to quit his job just yet. Before long, however, God would make it clear that that was precisely what he needed to do.

Late in 1958, when Luis was twenty-four years old, two Christians from America came to speak in Cordoba. Dick Hillis was a former missionary to China who had been imprisoned by the Communists there for two years. Ray Stedman was the pastor of a dynamic church in Palo Alto, California. Luis was curious to see a pastor from California so went to the meeting.

Afterward he noticed Pastor Stedman standing alone and introduced himself in English. He was amazed when the pastor immediately asked him a lot of questions and seemed truly interested in him. Luis shared all about himself – his job, family, and evangelistic ministries. He was flattered when Pastor Stedman invited him to a Bible study with a few missionaries the next day.

Not until years later did Stedman reveal something remarkable to Luis: When the pastor first saw Luis, the Lord impressed on his heart to see that this young man got to the United States. Stedman did not know why, or, at that initial moment, even who the young man was. When he learned that Luis was actively involved in evangelism, he knew his leading was from the Lord.

Luis had a small motorbike on which he rode to work at the bank. After the Bible study at the missionary's house the following day, he offered to take Pastor Stedman into town on his motorbike to do a little necessary shopping. As they did so, Stedman continued to pepper Luis with questions. 'Would you like to go to seminary?' he asked.

'It would be nice, but I'm not sure I'll ever make it,' Luis answered honestly. 'I don't have a lot of money, and I need to take care of my family.'

'Well, it could be arranged if the Lord wanted it,' Stedman stated matter-of-factly. He then asked further, 'How would you like to come to the United States?'

'I've thought about it,' Luis revealed. 'Maybe someday I'll be able to go, the Lord willing.'

Luis thought the pastor was simply carrying on a polite conversation. It never occurred to him that a minister from the United States would be able to arrange for him to come there for further education. But Stedman again stated seriously, 'You know, Luis, the Lord may just will it.'

When Luis saw Stedman off at the airport the next day, the pastor was even more definite about his coming to the United States for his education: 'God is going to will it. The money will come for you and your mother. Don't worry. It is the Lord's will that you come.'

Not many days later Luis received a letter from Stedman, stating that he knew a businessman who wanted to pay for his trip to the United States so he could study at a well-known seminary there. Luis wrote back and thanked the pastor but declined his offer. 'I do not want to spend four more years in school,' he explained, 'while people are going to hell.' To himself he wondered, 'And who would take care of my family?'

Stedman immediately sent another letter, assuring Luis that someone from the United States would be able to provide for his family too. Luis was unsure how to respond to all this news, which sounded too good to be true. So he did not answer Stedman's letter for several months.

Meanwhile, other significant developments, both concerning and exciting, began to take place in Luis's life. At his job he needed to confront the bank manager about a few new practices that, while not illegal, were morally questionable. 'Due to my Christian testimony,' Luis informed the manager, 'I'm not sure I can do everything required of me.'

The manager was not at all pleased. He stated cooly: 'Let me remind you, Luis, of all the bank has done for you and all we have planned for you.' Rather than admitting that some of the bank's practices might be questionable, the manager hinted that Luis was putting his banking career at risk by rocking the boat.

The favor with which Luis was viewed at the bank immediately dropped. He realized that if he refused to do something the bank asked him to do, he would quickly be out of a job. He soon discovered, however, that all of this had happened in God's perfect timing.

A few days after his confrontation with the bank manager, Luis noticed an American opening a new account. Luis struck up a conversation with the man and soon learned that he was Keith Bentson, who served with SEPAL, the Latin American division of a larger missionary organization called Overseas Crusades.[2]

As Luis and Mr. Bentson talked, the missionary mentioned, 'I'm looking for a bilingual Christian man who might want to work for SEPAL, translating English material into Spanish for our magazine *La Voz* (The Voice).'

'You've got your man,' Luis immediately stated.

'Who?' Keith asked.

'It's me,' Luis replied with a smile. As soon as the missionary mentioned the job, Luis was certain it was for him.

'Oh, Luis,' Keith cautioned, 'you'd better think about it and talk with your family. We're talking about a very, very small salary; no doubt much less than you're making here at the bank.'

'I'll talk to my family,' Luis assured him, 'but I'm your man. This is exciting. I'm sure it's of God.'

Once Luis got over the shock of the tiny salary he would be paid by SEPAL, he felt on top of the world. He had finally found a way to get into full-time Christian

---

2 Overseas Crusades, which was later renamed OC International, had been founded and was led by Dick Hillis, the missionary speaker whom Luis had heard at a meeting with Ray Stedman.

work, which had long been the desire of his heart. He had not been so sure about God's leading in his life for a very long time.

Two of Luis's sisters had found jobs by that time, so having his salary cut by more than half did not affect the family too much. He loved all aspects of his ministry at SEPAL and continued his evangelistic preaching on his own time.

Luis's evangelistic ministry continued to grow. Bruce Woodman, a musically gifted missionary from America, volunteered to serve as part of Luis's evangelism team. Woodman was an excellent emcee, song leader and soloist for the outreach meetings.

In May of 1960, three SEPAL missionaries and Luis attempted to plant a new church within a short period of time in a location where no Christian worker had ever been before. They modeled their church planting effort after the Apostle Paul in the Book of Acts. God had used Paul to successfully plant new Christian congregations in previously unevangelized towns, often in very brief periods of time.

They carried out their church planting effort in Oncativo, a town of about 12,000 people, located some fifty miles from the city of Cordoba. Five Christians from a tiny church in Rio Segundo, several miles from Oncativo, agreed to be part of their church planting team. The Rio Segundo believers had never before ministered in Oncativo. The three missionaries let Luis and the other Argentine Christians take the lead in carrying out this ministry.

They held an impromptu rally in a park on May 25 and handed out hundreds of flyers announcing their evangelistic meetings. Then they 'prayed like crazy' that at least a small group of people would show up.

The only place in town they had found in which to hold their meetings was the storage room of a print shop. The room could hold only about seventy-five people. When it came time for the first meeting that night the room was packed.

Luis preached on John 10:28-29, where Jesus promised: 'I give them eternal life, and they shall never perish; no one can snatch them out of my hand. My Father, who has given them to me, is greater than all; no one can snatch them out of my Father's hand.'

Luis had never before given a public invitation, inviting people to publicly receive Christ as their Savior. That night he sensed both an inner compulsion and a complete freedom to do so. This was the first of thousands of public invitations he would give throughout his nearly six decades of evangelistic ministry to follow.

He asked everyone to bow their heads and, if they wanted to trust in Christ as their Savior, to pray along with him. He then led them through a simple salvation prayer. When he asked those who had prayed with him to raise their hands, thus signifying their decision to trust in Jesus, nearly three dozen people (about half the gathered group) did so.

Fearing they may have misunderstood, Luis said, 'Let me explain again.' He then spent another half hour reviewing the same Scripture passage he had just preached on, seeking to make sure each point was completely clear. When he again led people in prayer for salvation and asked those who had done so to raise their hand, even more hands went up!

The evangelism team held meetings every night, and seventy people professed faith in Christ that week. The evangelists also trained the new Christians so they could form their own church. They taught them about baptism, communion, witnessing, teaching God's Word, and becoming reliable church leaders.

The five believers from Rio Segundo were spiritually revived through that week of ministry. They committed themselves to watch over the new church in Oncativo as if it were made up of their own sons and daughters. Over the next couple of years, the Christians in Rio Segundo and Oncativo went out and planted several other churches in neighboring towns.

Bible School, Marriage, and Becoming a Missionary

Ray Stedman had continued to write Luis, encouraging him to come to the United States for further Bible training. Pastor Stedman assured the enthusiastic young evangelist that he would not need to set aside his evangelistic ministry for four long years while studying in seminary. Instead, Stedman told Luis about a one-year graduate-level Bible training program at Multnomah School of the Bible in Portland, Oregon, that might perfectly suit his educational needs and desires.[1]

The pastor also sent money for Luis's mother, as a token of how they intended to help support her while he pursued his education. She encouraged her son to take advantage of this splendid opportunity and to trust God to provide for himself and his family.

All this at last persuaded Luis to go to the U.S. for further Bible training. He began attending Multnomah School of the Bible the fall semester of 1960. He greatly enjoyed his classes and was 'treated royally' by his fellow students and teachers.

---

1 A graduate-level program is taken after a person has completed college. The school was later named Multnomah Bible College and Biblical Seminary.

However, unknown to others, he struggled deeply with feelings of being a hypocrite. He sincerely desired to be the strong, spiritual Christian who others perceived him to be and who he himself longed to be. Instead, he seemed to wrestle constantly with his own envy, self-centeredness, and ambition to succeed and gain recognition for himself.

An anonymous friend of Ray Stedman had paid for Luis's first semester of schooling. But Luis became so discouraged with himself, it seemed hopeless to dream that God or anyone else would give him ten dollars, let alone pay for another half year of his education. 'As soon as the semester is over,' he decided, 'I'm going back to Argentina.'

On Thanksgiving weekend in late November, however, he found a plain envelope with his name on it in his school mailbox. It contained an unsigned, typed letter. He had no way of knowing who it was from.

Opening it, he was amazed to read: 'Dear Luis, you have been a great blessing to many of us here in the States, and we appreciate what you have taught us. We feel that you deserve help to finish your year at Multnomah. Therefore, all your tuition and books have been paid for.'

Luis was filled with gratitude, joy and relief for this generous and timely provision of his financial need. It also assured him that God was still with him after all, even with the spiritual defeat and frustration he had been experiencing.

Shortly before the first semester ended in December, one of the school chapel speakers was Major Ian Thomas. Major Thomas was a respected British evangelist, Bible teacher and Christian writer. He had established and directed the Capernwray Hall Bible School in England as well as Torchbearers International, a group of Bible Schools and Christian conference centers located around the world.

Major Thomas, who had received awards for his great courage in battle during World War II, spoke rapidly and with a strong British accent. His chapel message was only twenty-two minutes long, but it was used of God to completely change Luis's outlook on his spiritual life and service.

The Major based his short sermon that day on Exodus 3, where God appeared to Moses in a burning bush. 'It took Moses forty years of tending sheep in the wilderness,' Thomas stated, 'to realize that he was nothing.' The preacher further declared: 'God was trying to tell Moses, "I don't need a pretty bush or an educated bush or an eloquent bush. Any old bush will do, as long as I am in the bush. If I am going to use you, I am going to use you. It will not be you doing something for me, but me doing something through you."'

As Luis listened to the message, he realized that he was like a worthless, dried-up bush that could do nothing for God. Everything in his ministry was worthless unless God was in the bush. Only God could make something positive happen in his Christian life and ministry.

'I once imagined,' Major Thomas admitted, 'that because I was an aggressive, winsome, evangelistic sort of Christian, God could use me. But God didn't use me until I came to the end of myself.' When the major said that, Luis thought: 'That's exactly my situation. I am at the end of myself.'

Major Thomas closed his message by citing Galatians 2:20: 'I have been crucified with Christ; it is no longer I who live, but Christ who lives in me; and the life I now live in the flesh I live by faith in the Son of God, who loved me and gave Himself for me' (RSV).

As soon as the chapel service ended, Luis ran back to his dorm room in tears and fell to his knees next to his bunk. 'Lord, now I get it,' he prayed. 'I understand. The whole thing is "not I, but Christ in me". It's not what I'm going to do for You, but rather what You're going to do through me.'

Luis realized that in his personal spiritual life and service for the Lord he could not depend on himself or even on the many privileges and opportunities God had given him throughout his life. While he could use those privileges, he could not depend on them for his spiritual success. Rather, he needed to depend on the almighty Lord Jesus Christ, who was living in him. Christ would provide him with the power and everything else he needed for faithful, fruitful Christian living and service.

During that first semester at Bible school Luis met and was attracted to Patricia Scofield. Pat was a kindergarten teacher from nearby Beaverton, Oregon, who was studying at Multnomah to become an overseas missionary. Two years younger than Luis, she was mature, smart, and spiritually sensitive.

They were unofficially engaged by Valentine's Day of the following year, 1961. Their wedding took place at Pat's home church of Cedar Mill Bible Church near Portland not quite six months later, on August 5. Pat and her parents, Willard and Elsie Scofield, had attended that church from around the time they came to faith in Christ when Pat was a young girl. Pat received Jesus as her Savior at age eight.

Shortly after their wedding, Luis and Pat were approved to serve as missionaries with Overseas Crusades in Colombia, South America. In preparation for their future service in missions, they completed a seven-month missionary training internship program in Detroit, Michigan.

Then for two and a half months they worked as volunteers for Billy Graham's evangelistic campaign in Fresno, California, which took place in July 1962. This gave Luis the opportunity to see firsthand how a large city-wide evangelism crusade was organized and carried out.

At a breakfast for campaign staff and local supporters the week before the Fresno crusade meetings began, Luis and Pat were seated beside Mr. Graham. During the meal the conversation turned to Luis's desire to carry out mass evangelism meetings of his own in the future. Graham then gave Luis one of the most important pieces of advice he ever received, and it helped shape his ministry career.

Looking him straight in the eye, Graham advised: 'Go to the big cities, Luis. Don't take too much time in the smaller towns. The big cities are like the tall mountains. When it rains on top of the mountain, the water flows downhill and waters every valley. The mountain is the city. When the gospel rains there, it blesses the other places. But like water, it hardly ever flows uphill.'

During the crusade meetings, Luis was Graham's interpreter to the Spanish-speaking people in attendance. Meeting in a separate location from the main platform where Graham was preaching, Luis listened to the prominent evangelist through a radio headset, then translated into a microphone for the Spanish-speaking audience. 'How thrilling to be a small part of the conversions that week!' Luis later commented.

That same summer Luis became a full-fledged U.S. citizen, and Pat discovered she was expecting their first child. They were shocked when, in January 1963, Pat gave birth to twins rather than the one baby they had been anticipating. The boys, Kevin and Keith, arrived two months early and weighed less than four pounds apiece at birth. They needed to stay in the hospital for five weeks but then were able to return home and grew into healthy children.

Early the following year, 1964, the Palaus went to Costa Rica, where Pat completed her Spanish language training. That summer they arrived in Bogota, the capital of Colombia, to begin their missionary service with Overseas Crusades.

Learning that the city of Cali was reportedly more receptive to the Christian gospel, Luis and a few other missionaries began working with a Christian and Missionary Alliance Church there. When they started holding evangelistic street preaching meetings, the local Christians did not want to get involved. Luis could not blame them, because the situation in Colombia was uncertain for Protestant believers.

For more than a decade, gospel-believing Christians had been severely persecuted for their faith; scores had even been killed. Street preaching was simply not done. Still, change seemed to be in the air, and the missionaries were convinced God was about to open wide the door for evangelism in Colombia.

Bruce Woodman, who had earlier served with Luis in Argentina, had since begun ministering at HCJB Radio, a far-reaching Christian radio station in Quito, Ecuador. Mr. Woodman invited Luis to travel to Quito occasionally to record a series of daily evangelistic radio programs. Later they started a series of daily Bible teaching programs as well. For decades both those programs continued to be broadcast on hundreds of radio stations and were heard daily by an estimated twenty-two million Spanish-speaking people. Many of those individuals were won to faith in Christ while others were built up in their Christian faith through the broadcasts.

Luis knew Overseas Crusades (OC) wanted him to be 'a regular missionary' who trained local Christians in evangelism and church planting. Yet he passionately desired to start carrying out mass evangelism. He kept writing to the OC home office, asking permission to begin that type of ministry. Whenever Dick Hillis, the OC President, or one of the mission's other board members visited Colombia, Luis would privately plead with them to let him start his own evangelism team and begin holding evangelistic crusades.

'I'm now thirty years old,' the earnest young missionary would state, 'and I feel as if good opportunities for mass evangelism are beginning to slip by me. There's no time to waste. Millions of people are dying without hearing the gospel and going to hell. I must take the message of salvation to them.'

While appreciating Luis's eagerness to start proclaiming the gospel on a large scale, the OC leaders revealed to him: 'We have started you in a small ministry because you still have many things to learn, including a fuller degree of humility. We're not ready to turn you loose for mass crusades just yet.'

Looking back many years later, Luis would comment on this earlier time in his ministry: 'It seemed logical to me that OC should allow such a crusade team within the mission, but they weren't sure I was ready for it yet. And they were probably right. At least my wife, Pat, thought so!'

The first local church campaign Luis was assigned to supervise was at La Floresta Presbyterian Church in Cali, in September 1965. He knew if their outreach strategy was going to work in large citywide crusades, it would also need to work in small local churches. La Floresta qualified as that, having only about sixty members.

Luis's plan was to spend the first week of the training campaign addressing the spiritual condition of the church people. There would be no use trying to mobilize Christians to carry out evangelism and discipleship if they had not first confessed known sin, dedicated themselves to the Lord, and begun enjoying a life that was centered on Christ and guided by God's Holy Spirit.

Luis was confident that his training program was spiritually sound and beneficial. However, he was not prepared for a dramatic work of God that interrupted his intended training for a time. 'Eventually we got it all in,' he afterward related, 'but I nearly didn't get past the second night [of training]. Spiritual revival broke out!'

As God's Spirit worked mightily in the congregation, scores of people got right with the Lord, confessing their sins. In just two weeks' time more than 125 individuals trusted Christ as Savior. Around eighty of those joined that church. For months on end the church continued in a state of revival, overflowing with joy and spontaneous evangelism.

During the initial two weeks of the revival, Luis could hardly sleep. 'Several of us walked around town at night, too excited to sleep,' he later reported. 'We were praying and dreaming big dreams for the future: If God can do this in one local church, what else can He do?'

Maria's Story of Tragedy and Triumph

In November of that year, Luis returned to Quito to test a new ministry idea. He hosted live Christian counseling television programs. People phoned in to the television studio, and Luis offered them guidance from the Bible to help them with their questions and problems in life. In addition, he shared the gospel of salvation with the callers, pointing them to Jesus as the ultimate solution to their spiritual needs, not only in this life but also for eternity.

These phone counseling sessions were broadcast live on television. Luis started with a short television program. But so many people phoned in, even after each program ended, that after two weeks Luis stayed on the air three hours at a time.

All types of people with many different kinds of problems phoned for advice. One person would be going through a financial crisis. Another was having a painful family problem. A third was thinking about committing suicide. Yet another was under heavy conviction for his own sin.

One night Luis received a phone call that led to one of the strangest and most dramatic visits he would ever

have with a person throughout all his many years of
ministry. That evening one of the people who phoned
Luis simply requested an appointment to speak to him
in-person at 9:30 the next morning. The caller spoke
in a 'tiny, high-pitched, squeaky voice.' When Luis
agreed, the person with the squeaky voice thanked him
and immediately hung up.

Promptly at the agreed-upon time the following
morning, Luis spotted a small woman walking through
the gates of the HCJB property. She was accompanied
by two huge men who looked like American football
players to Luis.

As she entered the office, Luis asked, 'Would your
two friends like to come in also?'

'No,' she said. 'One will stand by the door and the
other by the gate.' Hers was the squeaky voice from
the abrupt phone call of the night before.

After brushing past Luis, the woman felt along the
bottom edges of his desk, as if she was looking for
something. She then peeked behind a hanging picture
on the wall. Her eyes inspected every corner of the
room before she finally sat down. Luis thought she
must be mentally imbalanced.

She swore and smoked unlike anyone Luis had
ever met. She sneered and her tiny voice dripped with
sarcasm and hatred.

'You pastors and priests,' she began with obvious
disgust, 'are a bunch of thieves and liars and crooks. All
you want is to deceive people. All you want is money.'

For the next twenty minutes she continued on without a single break, accusing and insulting while swearing constantly. Luis had no idea how to respond to her and could not have gotten a word in, even if he had tried. 'Lord, how shall I handle this?' he silently prayed.

Finally, the woman slumped in her chair, as if exhausted from her outburst. Her eyes were still flashing with anger. As she paused to take a deep breath, Luis asked: 'Madam, is there anything I can do for you? How can I help you?'

She slowly took her cigarette from her lips and sat staring at him for a moment. Then she suddenly burst into uncontrollable sobs. After she had composed herself and could speak again, the anger and bitterness were gone from her voice. 'You know,' she revealed, 'in the thirty-eight years I have lived, you are the first person who has ever asked me if he could help me. All my life people have come to me with their hands out, saying, "Help me. Come here, do this. Go there, do that."'

'What is your name?' Luis asked.

She immediately seemed suspicious, asking, 'Why do you want to know my name?'

'Well, you've said a lot of things here, and I don't even know you. I just want to know how to address you.'

She cocked her head, then looked at Luis out of the corner of her eye, as though she was trying to decide whether it was safe to identify herself. 'I'm going to tell you,' she at last said decidedly. 'My name is Maria Benitez-Perez.' Luis immediately recognized her last name as that of a large family of wealth and influence. 'I am the secretary of the Communist Party here in Ecuador. I do not believe in God.'

She then launched into another breathless, angry tirade against all preachers and priests, the Bible, the church, and anything else she could think of that opposed her beliefs. After a while she said, 'I'm going to tell you my story.' For the next three hours she did so without pause or interruption.

She had been a rebellious teenager who ran away from a religious school. When her parents gave her the choice of returning to school or leaving the family, she left. The Communists befriended her and provided for her. Over the next few years she was married and divorced three times and had several children. She also became a Communist Party leader and organized student rebellions.

Maria shared her communist beliefs, as well as her opposition to everything that Christianity stood for. Then, however, she most unexpectedly asked: 'Listen, Palau, supposing there is a God. And I'm not saying there is, because I don't believe in the Bible, and I don't believe there's a God. But just for the sake of chatting about it, if there is a God – which there isn't – do you think He would receive a woman like me?'

Luis opened his Bible to Hebrews 10:17, which states, 'Their sins and their lawless deeds I will remember no more.' Turning the Bible so Maria could see it, he said: 'Look, Maria, don't worry about what I think; look at what God thinks.'

'But I don't believe in the Bible,' she objected.

'You've already told me that,' Luis replied. 'But we're just supposing there's a God, right? Let's just suppose this is His Word. He says, "Their sins and their lawless deeds I will remember no more."'

She waited, as if she expected Luis to say more. When he said nothing, she responded: 'But listen. I've been an adulteress, married three times, and in bed with a lot of different men.'

'"Their sins and their lawless deeds I will remember no more,"' Luis quoted the verse again. He began counting the number of times he repeated it.

'I haven't told you half my story,' Maria asserted. She continued to recount one very serious transgression after another which she had committed: 'I stabbed a comrade who later committed suicide. I've led student riots where people were killed. I egged on my friends and then hid while they were out dying for the cause.'

Seventeen times Luis responded to Maria's confessions and objections by reciting that one Bible verse. At last, he asked her: 'Would you like Christ to forgive all that you've told me about, and all the rest that I don't even know?'

Maria was quiet for a time as she pondered the question. Then she said softly: 'If He could forgive me and change me, it would be the greatest miracle in the world.'

Luis led her in a simple salvation prayer. By the end of the prayer, she was in tears.

Maria returned a week later to tell Luis that she was reading the Bible and felt much better. A missionary from HCJB agreed to study the Bible with her, to help her grow in her new Christian faith.

Two months later, in January 1966, Luis returned to Quito to record more radio programs and to do more spiritual counseling on television. When Maria came to visit him, he was shocked at her appearance. Her face was covered with bruises and several of her front teeth were missing.

Maria now told Luis that shortly after trusting in Christ, she had informed her comrades about her new Christian faith. At a meeting with all the Communist leaders of the country, she courageously told them: 'I am no longer an atheist. I believe in God and in Jesus Christ. I have become a Christian. I am resigning from the party, and I don't want to have anything more to do with it. We are all a bunch of liars. We deceive people when we tell them there is no God.'

The Communist leaders argued among themselves. Some tried to shout her down and to hurt her, while another insisted she should be allowed to speak. A few days later she was nearly run down by a jeep full of her former comrades. The next day several of the university students whom she had earlier helped to train in carrying out violence and rebellion attacked her. They smashed her face against a utility pole until she was unconscious.

After that she had to hide out in several church basements and in the homes of missionaries. Before she and the HCJB missionary could study the Bible together, they first had to drive around until they were sure no one was following them. Luis was amazed at the persecution Maria had endured as a young Christian.

She stayed true to her Christian faith. On one occasion she even had the unexpected opportunity to share with the chairman of the Communist Party in Ecuador about her faith in Jesus and how He had changed her life. She encouraged the Communist leader to believe in God and in Jesus His Son.

Beginning Mass Evangelism Ministry

In December of 1966, Luis went to Bogota, Colombia, to preach the gospel in a four-day evangelistic campaign. This series of meetings had been planned by a national organization of Christian young people who wanted to make a spiritual impact on the country. Luis and the Colombian Christians realized this could bring strong opposition to them or, if the Lord blessed, could open their country to the gospel.

Thousands of Christians from surrounding towns were invited to participate in a huge parade that was to begin the evangelistic outreach. 7,000 Christian young people walked in rows that stretched out for twelve city blocks. As they walked, each person held the Bible over his or her heart, signifying their allegiance to God's Word.

Everyone also carried small transistor radios. The campaign leaders had purchased radio time from one of the local stations so a selection of Christian songs could be broadcast during the march. The parade participants tuned into the music on that station and sang together as they walked along.

'It was impressive but dangerous,' Luis afterward revealed. 'To be honest, I was frightened.'

Shortly after the parade got underway, the Christians saw red lights flashing and knew that police cars were coming. Many feared that law officials were coming to make arrests. However, when the patrol cars reached the front of the parade, they took positions leading the march, with their red lights still flashing to help clear the avenue for the procession.

The atmosphere in the parade became joyous, with the songs being sung more loudly. Posters and banners with Bible verses swung enthusiastically in the air. Many older Christians, including a group of missionaries and national pastors, joined the procession. Even half a dozen Catholic priests and a group of nuns joined in.

The parade had swelled to 12,000 participants by the time it reached Bolivar Plaza, a huge square bordered by government offices and the city's main cathedral. 20,000 people had jammed into the plaza by the time Luis was to speak. Standing on the stairway of the main government building, he preached on 'Christ the Liberator' from John 8:36: 'So if the Son makes you free, you will be free indeed.'

At the end of his brief message, 300 people raised their hands to publicly indicate their decision to trust in Jesus as their Savior. More than 550 other individuals made public commitments to Christ during the evangelistic meetings over the next four nights. Attendances at the Bogota meetings totaled 42,000.

After Luis's four years of missionary training and service with Overseas Crusades, the mission organization invited him to become its field director for the country of Mexico and to set up his headquarters there. OC also gave him its encouragement and blessing to develop his own evangelism team with the purpose of reaching that country with the gospel. Luis was thrilled to at last be able to pursue his long-time desire of carrying out mass evangelism.

The Palaus began their ministry in Mexico in the middle of 1968. That year Luis also returned to Colombia to conduct evangelistic campaigns in three cities. Those meetings lasted for nineteen days and were attended by 41,300 people. Nearly 1,600 of those individuals publicly placed their faith in Jesus.

The following year Luis and his team held evangelistic campaigns in seven cities in Mexico. Those meetings stretched out for 104 days and had 104,500 attendees. Even more importantly, 7,360 people registered public commitments to Christ.

The largest of those Mexico campaigns was held in a bullring in Monterrey. More than 30,000 people heard the gospel there in nine days, and 2,000 individuals responded to the public invitations that were given.

A young pastor and his tiny congregation were heavily involved in the Monterrey campaign. The church was located in a rough neighborhood notorious for drugs and muggings. Church people brought everyone they could to the meetings, including drug addicts and prostitutes. Fifteen new families were added to the church through the campaign. One drug addict who was converted through the church's witness later became the pastor of a church in a neighboring city.

A set of large meetings that Luis had planned to hold at a baseball park in Mexico City was canceled at the last minute by the government. As an alternate plan, the intended meetings were held in two of the oldest and most respected Protestant churches in the city. The two church buildings stood back-to-back. By staggering meeting times, Luis was able to close the service at one church and rush over to the other church just in time to start preaching again. God gave him the strength to maintain that rigorous schedule throughout the fifteen-day campaign, during which 2,000 people made public commitments.

One of the individuals who became a Christian during those Mexico City meetings was a university student named Carlos. He was a fanatical follower of Karl Marx and Vladimir Lenin, whose influential and radical teachings had led to the establishment of socialism and communism in many countries.

Carlos was interested in a quiet, sweet young lady he had met at the university. She invited him to attend a youth meeting with her, which he happily did in order to spend time with her. He did not realize this was one of the youth meetings Luis was holding as part of the Mexico City crusade. When the young people started singing Christian choruses, Carlos nearly stomped out of the meeting.

However, he decided to stay, and the Lord dramatically changed his heart and life through the gospel message he heard that day. Luis afterward described Carlos's instant conversion this way: 'In one sweeping strike the Holy Spirit swept him that very hour into the kingdom of God.'

Carlos immediately rejected communism due to its opposition to Christ and Christianity. He joined a local church, was baptized, and received training to grow as a follower of Jesus. Remarkably, as a zealous young Christian he led more than 120 people to Christ while completing his psychology degree at the university.

Luis and Pat's family had continued to grow. Their third son, Andrew, was born in February 1966 and their fourth and final child, Stephen, arrived in November 1969.

Luis's evangelism team was growing too. During the late 1960s and early 1970s, dedicated team members were added from Ecuador, Guatemala, the United States, and other nations. They became the first evangelism team in Latin American history to be made up of individuals from several different nations and church denominations.

In 1970 Luis and his team returned to Mexico City for another campaign. They had heard that another religious group had drawn a large crowd to a 'convention' in the city. So this time Luis's team called their Mexico City crusade a convention. Not wanting city authorities to shut down their public meetings again, as had happened the year before, Luis's team advertised only on their radio programs and by word of mouth.

Despite those limitations, more than 106,000 people attended the ten-day crusade, and 6,670 individuals made public decisions. Some churches doubled in size almost overnight. It was the greatest response Luis and his team had ever seen to the gospel, and they were overjoyed.

The 1970 Mexico City campaign attracted the attention of many Christians to what God was doing in that part of the world. Just as Billy Graham had been holding large, fruitful evangelistic crusades in America and other countries, so now similar results were taking place in Luis's campaigns in South America. One journalist reporting on the Mexico City crusade called Luis 'the Billy Graham of Latin America.' The designation took hold, and Luis came to commonly be referred to in that way.

Luis's team always recorded the number of public decisions made at his crusade meetings. They did this in order that God would be praised for the important spiritual work He was doing in so many people's lives. Luis's team also sent helpful Christian literature to those who responded to the public invitations, to encourage them in the commitments they had made to Christ.

Usually more than half the people who made public decisions did so to receive Jesus as their Savior. Sometimes far more than half made first-time salvation commitments. Others who responded to the invitations did so to gain assurance of their salvation or to rededicate their lives to the Lord. God knew the specific spiritual decision that every person was making, and each commitment was extremely important.

Other salvation and rededication decisions were made in the hearts of some people who did not respond to the public invitations. In addition, countless other individuals were led to saving faith in Jesus outside of the crusade meetings, by friends and relatives who had become Christians or rededicated their lives to Christ during the campaign.

Reaching All Latin America
for Christ

Late in 1970, Luis and his team were making advance preparations to hold a large campaign in Lima, the capital of Peru, the following year. At that time Peru was not a safe, stable country. A military dictatorship had seized control of the nation, and communist rebels were trying to overthrow the government. Many rebels were carrying out guerrilla warfare (irregular, undercover fighting). Bloodshed was common in parts of the country.

Luis was invited to preach at some pre-crusade rallies in Lima in December 1970. At one of those meetings, a communist revolutionary named Rosario came with the intention of attacking him or perhaps ending his life!

Rosario was born out of wedlock in the slums outside Lima. She grew up full of anger at the lack of food and water as well as the poverty she saw all around her.

Although she did not finish her formal education, she became an avid reader. By age thirteen she was reading the works of Marx and Lenin. By the time she was eighteen she had become a militant communist.

She hated the upper classes and anyone else whom she thought stood in the way of communist ideals being set up in society. More than once on her missions, she had violently attacked or even killed her perceived opponents. She also hated anything that had to do with God or Christianity.

Rosario happened to hear one of Luis's Spanish radio programs and learned that he would be speaking live at a theater in Lima that evening. Though she knew nothing else about him, she was immediately filled with rage and hatred toward him.

That night Rosario sat in the auditorium, listening to Luis's message on 'The Five Hells of Human Existence' – murder, robbery, deceit, hypocritical homes, and hatred. Each sin he mentioned pricked her conscience. When he gave an invitation at the close of the sermon, she came forward with scores of other people. But murder rather than becoming a Christian was on her mind.

A little old lady, a Peruvian Christian, had come forward as well, to counsel anyone who might desire guidance in making a spiritual decision. Approaching Rosario, the older woman said, 'Madam, may I help you receive Christ?' Rosario struck the well-intentioned counselor, then panicked at the commotion she had caused and fled from the theater.

Later that night, as Rosario tossed and turned in bed, God's Spirit kept pressing two verses from Luis's message on her mind. The first, Jeremiah 17:5, states: 'Cursed is the one who trusts in man, who depends on flesh for his strength, and whose heart turns away from the Lord.' The contrasting verse, Jeremiah 17:7, says: 'Blessed is the man who trusts in the Lord, whose confidence is in him.'

Very early the next morning, Rosario fell on her knees and trusted in Christ Jesus to save her from her many sins. She stood back up a fully forgiven, completely changed child of God.

Previously Rosario tried to help the poor by forcing radical communist ideology on society, even through the use of violence. After her Christian conversion, she did even more to aid the poor, but now out of Christian compassion. Through her efforts, running water and electric lights were provided for the poor neighborhood where she had grown up.

She also met with factory bosses and admonished them to treat their employees fairly. 'I warn them,' she stated, 'that Christ is over them' (Colossians 4:1). She addressed high school classes and debated political issues, using her own experiences to show that only Christ can meet people's deepest needs. Scores of young people came to believe in Jesus as a result of her ministry.

Luis did not learn about Rosario's Christian conversion and subsequent service until he read her testimony in a German news service report, a full ten years after the initial Lima crusade of 1971. A few more years passed until he finally met her during another Lima campaign.

Luis correctly points out: 'Marxist revolutions in Latin America and elsewhere have never transformed lives for the better. As Rosario's story illustrates, the only revolution that works occurs every time someone becomes a new creation in Christ. He alone changes lives for good here and now – and for all eternity.'

When Luis returned to Lima a few months later, in 1971, for the full evangelistic crusade, 103,000 people attended the meetings held in the city's large bullring. Through the course of the two-week campaign, nearly 5,000 individuals made public commitments to Christ.

An important new development during that crusade was the large amount of positive publicity it received from the secular media. Previously, Christians had been ridiculed or simply ignored by the media in Peru. Suddenly the evangelistic campaign was receiving nationwide news coverage. Excerpts from Luis's messages were broadcast on forty-five radio stations.

This massive amount of media coverage brought another blessing as well. Luis and his team were able to reach even the highest levels of society.

In Guatemala that same year, the President of the country requested a personal interview with Luis. This provided the evangelist with the opportunity of a twenty-five-minute meeting with the President to discuss how Christianity builds a nation.

'How can it do that?' the country's leader asked.

'Primarily through people who have their lives changed through belief in Jesus Christ and the power of God's Word,' Luis explained. 'Those individuals live a just, hard-working life. They love their neighbors as they love themselves. When many people live like that by the power of God, the whole nation is strengthened.'

Luis and his ministry associates were also able to meet with the mayor of the capital, Guatemala City, with the U.S. Ambassador to Guatemala, and with the country's top military officers. Throughout the twenty-two-day crusade, Luis preached to 128,800 people, with more than 3,150 of them making public decisions.

Guatemala's leading newspaper provided thorough coverage almost every day of the meetings, even quoting Scripture that Luis referenced in his messages. Other news media throughout the country clamored for interviews. One of Luis's radio interviews was broadcast more than sixty times on eight separate national stations in a single day. An English-speaking church raised enough money to pay for ten weekly gospel programs to be broadcast on secular television immediately after the campaign ended.

Other notable campaigns carried out during the early 1970s included: Honduras, 1971 (57,000 attendees, 2,434 decisions); Costa Rica, 1972 (62,500 attendees, 3,205 decisions); Guatemala, 1972 (115,000 attendees, 3,197 decisions); Dominican Republic, 1973 (71,600 attendees, 2,373 decisions).

'This is the hour of God in Spanish America!' became the watchword (core aim and belief) of Luis and his team. 'The twenty-three Spanish-speaking countries of Latin America are our parish," they told people. In stating that, they were echoing John Wesley, the great Methodist evangelist of the 1700s, who had declared, 'The world is my parish.'[1]

Publicly Luis's ministry organization announced the goal which they believed God had given them: 'To preach Jesus Christ fully to 250 million Spanish speaking people in the world within the decade [the 1970s], utilizing all communications media, so millions will be transformed into victorious Christians.'

Even Cuba, which was officially 'closed' to the gospel due to the Communist Government in power there, was being reached by Christian radio broadcasts.

Luis's team also started producing gospel films, which could be used by local churches in their outreach efforts and by missionaries starting new congregations. 'We can't bring 250 million Spanish people to a bullring to hear the gospel,' they realized. 'But we can take the same transforming message from a bullring to millions of people all across the continent.'

In the spring of 1974, Luis's team went to La Paz, the capital of Bolivia, to make preparations for a trio of evangelistic crusades in that country later in the year. During their springtime visit, the nation's first-ever Presidential Prayer Breakfast was held. At that same time Bolivia was being rocked by 100 percent increases in food costs, riots, an enormous rainstorm

---

1 A parish is the area in which a church's attendees live and the region to which they seek to minister.

and flooding, as well as a government crisis in which three members of the President's cabinet resigned.

At the prayer breakfast Luis spoke to 125 dignitaries, including the Bolivian President – General Hugo Banzer – and several other of the country's highest-ranking politicians, judges and military leaders. 'Never give up the battle for righteous government,' Luis challenged the President and his distinguished guests.

From the Bible he showed that it is impossible to govern a nation without God, emphasizing 2 Chronicles 7:14: 'If my people, who are called by my name, will humble themselves and pray and seek my face and turn from their wicked ways, then will I hear from heaven and will forgive their sin and will heal their land.' Luis then poured out his heart in prayer for Bolivia.

Afterward, President Banzer asked what he could do to help Luis's team reach his nation with the Christian gospel. The evangelist boldly asked for ten nights of free airtime on national television, beginning that very evening with their normal live call-in counseling program. The President readily agreed.

On the way to the television studios, Luis chatted with Chester Schemper, South American director of The Bible League. 'What we really need,' Luis suggested to Schemper, 'is 3,000 of your New Testaments to give away to the TV viewers who call in to our program.'

'And who's going to pay for them?' Schemper asked.

'All your rich American supporters!' Luis responded with a smile.

The next morning President Banzer phoned a missionary friend of Luis's who served in Bolivia, David Farah. 'I was watching Palau on television last night,' the President informed David. He then stunned the missionary by stating: 'If you can get me one million copies of the New Testament, I will pass them on to the Ministry of Education! Instead of having catechism classes, we will have everyone studying the New Testament.'

David reported to Luis what the President had said, and they both talked to Chester Schemper. In a huge step of faith that the Lord would provide the necessary money, The Bible League agreed to supply the one million New Testaments. Consequently, starting in 1975 all primary and secondary school students in Bolivia studied the New Testament twice a week.

As planned, Luis's team returned to Bolivia in the fall of 1974 to hold crusades in three cities. A total of 82,400 people attended the three weeks of meetings. God's Spirit worked powerfully in people's hearts, and 9,210 individuals made public decisions. That was more than had ever responded publicly to Luis's invitations during a campaign.

That same year Luis conducted a campaign in Netzahualcoyotl, a fast-growing metropolis near Mexico City. A huge 'canvas cathedral' was filled to overflowing for the meetings that were held that week. To the 'utter amazement' of Luis and his team, two-thirds of the more than 1,400 people who made public commitments that week were teenage boys and men. Usually older boys and men were least likely to commit their lives to Christ.

Luis next returned to Ecuador for a three-week crusade in the capital city of Quito. The campaign started very slowly, with low attendances at the first five days of meetings. After that, Luis and the executive committee overseeing the crusade met to announce they were canceling the third week of meetings.

However, the determined group of Christian leaders from Quito who were working with Luis's team in having the campaign strongly protested shortening the intended crusade. 'The local committee clobbered me,' Luis revealed afterward, 'exhorting and forcing me to consent to go the whole way.'

At first Luis and his team members shook their heads at being pressured into going on with all the meetings. But by the end of the campaign, they were glad they had stuck it out. The Bible Society sold out its entire stock of 10,000 Spanish Bibles and 7,000 New Testaments several days before the crusade ended. Attendances climbed to 10,000 some nights, with an overall campaign attendance of 79,900. Most importantly, 3,120 people indicated their decision to follow Jesus as Savior and Lord. Remarkably, nine out of ten of those individuals had not previously heard the salvation message.

First Evangelistic Campaigns in Europe

In 1974 Luis traveled to Sevilla, Spain, to hold his first European crusade. Sevilla's six evangelical churches invited Luis to come for the first-ever public evangelistic campaign in the city's history.

The Spanish Inquisition[1] had started in Sevilla five centuries earlier. While such persecution had not been practiced in Spain for many years, Spanish law did not officially allow religious freedom until just eight years before Luis's ministry in the country.

For decades Christian missionaries in Spain had planted the seeds of God's Word, but with little spiritual fruit. Of Sevilla's population of 750,000, less than 500 claimed to be born-again Christians. Luis and his team, therefore, joyously praised God when more people professed faith in Jesus as Savior each night of the crusade than had received Christ in many years.

Another ministry highlight for Luis in 1974 was the publication of his first book, *Walk on Water, Pete!* The book, published in English and Spanish, was a series of spiritual lessons from the example of the Apostle Peter.

---

1 When those who did not confess to be Roman Catholics were brutally persecuted.

This was the first of many helpful books that Luis would write throughout the years to follow.

During the summer of 1975 Luis, then forty years old, joined Billy Graham for Eurofest '75, which was held in Brussels, Belgium. They challenged 8,000 young people from more than thirty nations to 'reclaim Europe in Jesus's name.'

Luis presented the morning Bible message every other day throughout the conference. Those messages were simultaneously translated into thirteen languages.

That conference was also attended by young people from Israel and Egypt, some of whom had fought each other's countries in Israel's Six-Day War just two years earlier. Reconciliation took place at the conference, with Christians from both sides embracing each other and asking for forgiveness.

That fall Luis conducted a three-week crusade in Managua, the capital of Nicaragua. This was his largest campaign to date, being attended by 187,000 people. Over 5,700 of those individuals made public decisions.

In conjunction with that campaign, Luis's team put together the most ambitious Christian communications network that had ever been attempted. Using a satellite and other technology, they broadcast the crusade messages on more than 150 radio and television stations from New York to Punta Arenas, Chile, the southernmost city in the world. In that one wide-sweeping evangelistic effort they reached some eighty million people with the gospel.

One evening near the end of the crusade Luis was on his way into Managua's brightly lit National Baseball Stadium. He was met by an older woman with tears in her eyes who gave him 'a big Latin hug.'

'Thank you for presenting the gospel so clearly,' she said to him. 'My grandson, Danilo, received the Lord several nights ago. The next morning he was so happy. He told me, "Granny, I've got eternal life." ' However, a day later tragedy struck.

Luis had been preaching through the Book of Romans during that campaign. He decided to change the focus of his next message, which he entitled, 'I'll See You in Heaven, Danilo'. He told Danilo's story just as the boy's grandmother had related it to him.

The day after Danilo accepted Christ he went out delivering newspapers. The audience thought the evangelist was going to report that the boy had invited his neighbors to the crusade that night. Instead, Luis stated, 'Then a truck came along, and pow!'

'Ohhh!' the crowd of some 30,000 people gasped. They were shaken by the unexpected news of Danilo's death, as Luis had been when the boy's grandmother first told him of it.

Luis then shared the teachings of Jesus Christ from the opening verses of John 14: 'Do not let your hearts be troubled. Trust in God; trust also in me. In my Father's house are many rooms; if it were not so, I would have told you. I am going there to prepare a place for you. And if I go and prepare a place for you,

I will come back and take you to be with me, that you also may be where I am. You know the way to the place where I am going. ... I am the way and the truth and the life. No one comes to the Father except through me' (verses 1-4, 6).

'I invite you,' Luis appealed to his audience, 'to believe in Jesus as your Savior, so you, like Danilo, can receive God's gift of eternal life. Then you, too, can have the joy of knowing that Christ has prepared a home for you in heaven, whenever your earthly life comes to an end.'

Many people responded to the gospel invitation that evening. In addition, millions of individuals heard that night's message via satellite and the continent-wide radio broadcast. Luis's organization also produced a Spanish film of that sermon, which pointed many others to faith in Christ.

Luis's sermons were always based on the Bible's teachings. He explained what the Scriptures meant in simple language that non-Christians could understand. He used real-life illustrations that people could easily relate to. While his overall tone was serious and earnest, he also mixed in a bit of good humor now and again.

Luis was an energetic speaker gesturing constantly with his hands and arms. Reporters described him as looking like a conductor waving his arms or a prizefighter moving agilely around the podium.

While Luis's invitation at the close of his message was very fervent, he did not play on people's emotions or try to whip up enthusiasm. He also did not attempt to pressure individuals into making a public decision. He simply appealed to people to come and get right with the Lord.

His favorite Bible verse to use in giving an invitation was Revelation 3:20, where Christ states: 'Behold, I stand at the door and knock; if anyone hears my voice and opens the door, I will come in to him and eat with him, and he with me' (RSV). Luis pictured Jesus at the door of people's hearts, being willing to come into their lives if they would believe and receive Him as Savior.

In the opening months of 1976, Luis carried out a pair of whirlwind ministry tours. One was to eight cities in Mexico in the span of just two weeks. He preached the gospel to over 111,000 people and saw 5,337 of them commit their lives to Christ.

That spring he had his first ministry tour in the United Kingdom where he spoke in thirteen British cities over the course of two weeks. He told one large, overflow audience: 'You cannot imagine what a joy and a privilege it is for me to visit the United Kingdom, to minister from the Word of God, to tell of His work in Latin America, and to say "thank you" to British Christians for their faithfulness in sending the missionaries who led my family and me to Jesus Christ.'

That summer Dick Hillis, the founding director of Overseas Crusades, asked the OC board to appoint Luis as his successor as president of the entire mission. After being assured that his new responsibilities with the mission would in no way hinder his ongoing ministries, Luis accepted the challenge.

Shortly after Luis and his team held a twelve-day campaign in Asuncion, the capital of Paraguay. Over 100,000 people were evangelized, with more than 4,900 making public commitments.

One of those individuals was a popular comedian in Paraguay. After watching Luis counsel people on television, he decided to host a mock call-in show on another station, to make fun of the evangelist. However, as he repeatedly listened to tapes of Luis's counseling programs to learn his mannerisms, the gospel message penetrated his heart. Rather than continuing to mock Christianity, he ended up surrendering his life to Jesus.

For over a year some members of Luis's team had been laying the foundation for a campaign in Rosario, Argentina. At first Luis was not eager to minister in that city which was notorious for its bombings, kidnappings, and murders in broad daylight.

It had taken ninety years of missionary activity for forty churches to be planted in Rosario. Most of those churches were small, isolated, and inwardly focused. Luis wondered if they could be brought together and motivated to help with a major outreach effort.

But Ed Silvoso, Luis's brother-in-law and one of his team members, was convinced that God was about to do a dramatic spiritual work in Rosario. Mr. Silvoso developed what became known as the 'Rosario Plan,' which was a vision to plant fifty new churches in just eighteen months. Those churches would be ready to receive new believers who came to faith in Christ during the upcoming evangelistic crusade.

Nearly seventy of the city's pastors and church leaders enthusiastically adopted the Rosario Plan. Their congregations caught the vision, became outwardly focused, and soon experienced a new spiritual vibrancy. Thirty-five home-based churches were planted.

During the November 1976 campaign, over 77,000 people attended the crusade meetings and nearly 5,200 placed their faith in Christ, thus doubling Rosario's number of born-again Christians in only a fortnight. In addition, over 110,000 homes throughout the city were visited, and hundreds of thousands heard the message of salvation by radio and television.

Extensive research carried out many months after the campaign revealed that over half the new Christian converts were incorporated into local churches and still living for the Lord. Thirty of the thirty-five new churches were still thriving spiritually three years later.

In the spring of 1977 Luis conducted his first crusade in Germany. The ten days of meetings were attended by 66,150 individuals. The German people were reserved about responding to Luis's public invitations, with 539 doing so. Still, the campaign was a good opportunity to proclaim the gospel in a country that greatly needed to hear it.

That summer Luis held a three-week campaign in Cardiff, Wales, in the southwest region of England.

Many years earlier Wales had experienced powerful spiritual revivals. By the 1970s, however, few Welsh people still held to Christian beliefs and practices.

Luis was somewhat taken aback by seemingly contradictory circumstances he observed in Wales: 'Paganized it was. I'd never seen anything like it anywhere else in the world. At every pub and sporting event, the Welsh – who love to sing – were packing down pints [of beer] as if they were going out of style, while singing gospel hymns with all the gusto they could muster. They absolutely loved the old hymns of the faith. But they simply did not know Jesus Christ.'

In Wales, Luis teamed up with British pop music star Cliff Richards. Richards was nearly as popular in Britain at that time as were the Beatles and Elvis Presley. Luis said of Richards: 'Cliff draws a crowd like few others can and puts out the gospel better than most. I rejoiced to hear him so clearly articulate [explain] the Christian faith he had made his own a few years earlier.'

One young woman admitted that she came to a crusade meeting solely to hear Cliff sing. When she stayed to listen to Luis's message, God's Spirit opened her heart and she was converted that night. Another young woman, a member of the Jehovah's Witnesses cult, came to faith in Jesus, and afterward led most of her family to Christ as well. Altogether nearly 1,600 people publicly committed themselves to Christ during the Cardiff campaign, which was attended by some 60,000 individuals.

Facing Atheists, Skeptics and Cancer

While much of South America was becoming more open to Christianity in the 1970s, one clear exception was Uruguay. Uruguay is located along the southeastern coast of the continent. Thirty percent of Uruguayans then claimed to be atheists, believing there is no God.

In 1978, Luis and his team members held evangelistic meetings in the capital of Montevideo and five other key cities scattered around Uruguay. Flying from city to city was not possible, so they instead traveled in an assortment of older cars, some of which seemed to require more oil than gas. They navigated across 1,600 miles of roads, which were often dusty and sometimes crowded with herds of cattle.

101,000 people attended the crusade meetings, with more than 8,100 publicly professing faith in Jesus. Seventy percent of those who trusted in Christ had been unchurched previously. 'I decided then and there,' Luis said afterwards, 'I like preaching to atheists!'

Two of the people who came to faith in Christ during the Montevideo campaign were an extremely unhappy married couple, Bario and Nancy, who had been planning to get a divorce. They no longer ate together and had not even spoken to each other for a very long time.

Nancy happened to see Luis on television, talking about family problems. 'Lord,' she cried out in her misery, 'if it's true that You exist, why are these things happening to me?' That night she informed Bario: 'Tomorrow I am going to the Palacio Penarol Stadium to hear Luis Palau speak.' Then she shuddered, realizing she had actually talked to her husband. They both ended up going to the crusade meetings and committed their lives and marriage to Christ.

'From that moment our lives have changed completely,' Nancy later reported. 'Every day we are surprised at how much we learn. We pray together and share things with each other. People say we aren't the same.' Within five months of their own Christian conversions, Bario and Nancy had been used of God to lead thirty-five other people to faith in Christ.

Not long after the Uruguay campaign Luis stepped down from being the president of Overseas Crusades, after two years of serving in that position. It was becoming impossible for him to effectively manage his own thirty-member evangelism team while at the same time providing the missionary organization with the leadership it needed.

All agreed that the time had come for the Luis Palau Evangelistic Association (LPEA) to become a separate missionary organization. Five months later, on October 1, the LPEA was officially launched with its own board of directors and its new headquarters in Beaverton, Oregon, near Portland. The LPEA was later renamed the Luis Palau Association (LPA).

For six years, since 1972, Luis and his team had published a quarterly news magazine in Spanish, called *Cruzada*, to share what God was doing through their evangelism ministries. Now in 1978, they launched *Continente Nuevo* for pastors and other Christian leaders throughout the Spanish-speaking world. In time, more than 40,000 leaders were receiving each issue of *Continente Nuevo*.

In October 1978, Luis returned to Bolivia, where four years earlier President Hugo Banzer requested and received one million Spanish New Testaments so God's Word could be taught in the nation's schools. The 1978 crusade meetings, held in the capital of La Paz and two other large cities, were attended by 180,000 people. Significantly, 18,916 individuals responded to the public invitations, more than twice the number to have done so in any previous campaign.

One of those who professed faith in Christ was Bolivia's new President, General Juan Pereda Asbun. Luis had the opportunity to share the good news of salvation with the President during a private meeting in his presidential office. There President Asbun bowed his head and prayed to receive Jesus as Savior and Lord.

During a press conference at a prestigious La Paz hotel that same week, Luis noticed when the eleven-year-old daughter of the hotel's elevator operator slipped into the meeting room. As she stood quietly nearby Luis, he thought she might desire a copy of one of the books he had written. He picked up one of them, autographed it, and handed it to her, while saying with a smile, 'The Lord bless you, sweetheart.'

'Mr. Palau,' the young girl responded unexpectedly, 'what I really wanted to ask you was how I could receive Jesus in my heart.' The previous evening she had watched the evangelist counsel people on national television. She had seen him lead a high school student to Christ and now desired to receive the Savior herself.

The press conference was brought to a hasty end, and the newsmen were asked to leave the room. Luis then prayed with the girl as she received Jesus. 'Publicity is necessary and fine,' Luis commented afterward, 'but the rest of their questions would have to wait until another time.' Quoting 2 Corinthians 6:2, he added: 'Now is the day of salvation.'

In the spring of 1979 Luis carried out his first evangelistic campaign in Australia. At the same time Billy Graham was conducting a crusade in Sydney, Luis was asked to hold meetings in Newcastle. Those four days of meetings were attended by 22,500 people but saw only 450 individuals respond publicly to the gospel invitations.

Luis was also able to speak at five universities. At the University of Sydney he addressed around 800 students on the campus's outdoor mall. As he attempted to speak on the theme of what Jesus Christ can do for a nation, a group of Marxist-Leninists began shouting disgusting and degrading remarks at him, trying to shut him down.

'You are reaping the benefits of living in a nation that has been blessed because of its Christian heritage,' Luis reminded the students. 'Benefits like freedom, fair laws, education, and a good degree of material prosperity.'

'Even when a nation has turned away from God and needs massive moral change,' Luis continued, 'there is only one revolution that works. That is the revolution in people's hearts and lives through faith in Christ Jesus.'

Those remarks led one angry young Marxist to point his finger at Luis and shout more immoral, offensive remarks at him. Luis tried to engage the young man in an intelligent conversation, but all the student seemed to know were swear words.

That same spring Luis and his team held a month-long campaign in a number of cities in northeast Scotland. 65,900 people attended those meetings and 1,364 made public decisions. For the first time, Luis's meetings received attention on local and national radio and television stations affiliated with the British Broadcasting Corporation (BBC).

Many in Britain thought that British society had permanently turned away from Christianity. 'Aren't you trying to flog a dead horse?' one BBC news reporter asked Luis.

'Why are you wasting your time on a post-Christian society?' another journalist queried him.

Luis's response likely surprised them: 'I don't believe there is any such thing as a post-Christian society. One generation may reject the gospel for itself. But each new generation has the opportunity to make its own choice. I cannot accept that a society can exist where the gospel is no longer relevant.'

His ten crusade messages in Aberdeen were broadcast nightly throughout Britain and Europe by a powerful Trans World Radio transmitter in Monte Carlo. Even Scottish ministers were surprised when they saw hundreds of people turning to Christ, including nearly 1,000 teenagers.

The following year Luis returned to Britain for a fast-paced evangelistic tour of England, sponsored by British Youth for Christ. In just two weeks' time he spoke at fifteen youth rallies in ten cities. 2,700 of the 30,000 attendees at those rallies registered commitments to Jesus Christ.

That same spring of 1980 Luis conducted a four-week, six-city campaign in Scotland. Those meetings attracted 62,500 attendees, 2,000 of whom responded to the public invitations.

Behind closed doors, a dozen Scottish ministers met with Luis to voice their opposition to organized mass evangelism efforts. 'We do not accept the Bible as the trustworthy Word of God,' fully half those particular ministers admitted to Luis.

'Was it any wonder their churches were faltering and failing?' Luis later asked. 'Who wants to listen to ministers who readily dismiss portions of Scripture?'

Shortly after that campaign it was discovered that Luis's wife, Pat, had breast cancer and needed surgery immediately. When the couple arrived at their home following the doctor's appointment in which they received that news, Luis went to his basement office to try to come to grips with this 'terrible blow.'

'This is the sort of thing that happens to other people,' he thought, 'but not to my wife. Not to Pat.' Many emotions welled up inside him, and he began to weep.

Suddenly his thoughts were interrupted by a familiar hymn being played on the piano. It took Luis's dazed mind a moment to realize that it was Pat herself who was playing the piano and singing 'How Firm a Foundation':

> How firm a foundation, ye saints of the Lord,
> Is laid for your faith in His excellent Word!
> What more can He say than to you He hath said,
> To you who for refuge to Jesus have fled?
>
> "Fear not, I am with thee; O be not dismayed,
> For I am thy God, and will still give thee aid;
> I'll strengthen thee, help thee, and cause thee to stand,
> Upheld by My righteous, omnipotent [all-powerful] hand.

'As the bottom was falling out of our lives,' Luis later reflected, 'the Lord reminded us both how desperately we needed to base our security and strength in Him alone.'

After her surgery, Pat underwent months of chemotherapy treatments, which left her feeling very weak and sick. Jeremiah 29:11 became one of her favorite Bible verses during that difficult time: ' "I know the plans I have for you," declares the Lord, "plans to prosper you and not to harm you, plans to give you hope and a future." '

For two years, planning had been underway for Luis's first full-scale evangelistic campaign in the United States. It was to be a Spanish-language crusade in Los Angeles. Elaborate arrangements for the campaign were already made and all the publicity had gone out.

Since Pat was still recovering from her recent surgery, Luis wondered if he and his team should cancel the Los Angeles crusade at the last minute. Pat, however, insisted that he should go ahead with it. Their two older sons, Kevin and Keith, were now seventeen years old and could stay home to help care for her. Luis could take their two younger sons, Andrew and Steve, ages fourteen and nearly eleven, with him to Los Angeles.

51,000 people attended the nine-day crusade in Los Angeles and 1,945 publicly committed their lives to Christ. Among them was a fourteen-year-old gang member who not long before had been treated at a hospital for gunshot and knife wounds.

Because of Pat's ongoing battle with cancer and difficult chemotherapy treatments, Luis held only two campaigns in 1981, rather than the half dozen or more he carried out most years. One of those was a demanding five-week crusade in Glasgow, Scotland.

Luis reminded his audiences there that at one time the city's motto was 'Let Glasgow flourish by the preaching of the Word and the praising of His Name.' Now its motto was simply 'Let Glasgow flourish'. Rather than flourishing, several well-known corporations had left the city and unemployment was high. Less than 4 percent of the population regularly attended church, and dozens of church buildings had closed in the past year.

Luis's team trained hundreds of committed Christians to be friendship evangelists. They agreed to regularly pray for five or ten family members, friends, and neighbors who had not yet trusted in Christ as Savior, then to invite them to the crusade meetings at Kelvin Hall.

One teenage girl rented a bus, believing she could fill it with friends to attend one of the meetings. However, when she invited her acquaintances, none of them accepted.

Shaken, she phoned the campaign prayer committee and asked them to pray about the situation. She then returned to her friends and convinced thirty-eight of them to attend the crusade with her. When Luis gave a public invitation, all thirty-eight were among those who went forward to make commitments to Christ.

Many other friendship evangelists reported seeing a few or several of their relatives and other acquaintances come to faith in Christ during the campaign. Altogether 198,000 people attended the Kelvin Hall meetings, and 5,325 of them registered public decisions during the thirty-six-day crusade.

That December a bone scan revealed that Pat had no further signs of cancer anywhere in her body. Luis, Pat, and their sons had an additional significant reason to celebrate that holiday season, as they thanked God for sparing her life.

Fruitful and Dangerous Ministries

The following year, 1982, Luis and his team carried out seven campaigns on four continents – North and South America, Australia, and Europe. In May they held a seven-day crusade in Helsinki, the capital of Finland. It was their first full-fledged crusade outside the Spanish and English-speaking worlds.

Later that year Luis was back in Guatemala City for a weeklong crusade held in conjunction with the centennial[1] celebration of the Christian gospel coming to the country of Guatemala. Christians from across the nation began flooding into the capital city. After sunrise that Sunday, they started making their way to Campo Marte, a gigantic empty military parade ground.

First tens of thousands, then hundreds of thousands of people began filling the park. Military helicopters flew overhead, trying to estimate the size of the crowd, which eventually swelled to some 700,000 individuals! It was the largest gathering of born-again Christians in the history of all Latin America.

It was also by far the largest number of people Luis had ever addressed in-person in a single gathering. More

---

1 A hundred years.

than a dozen radio stations broadcast his message live that day, allowing the 'vast sea of people' at the meeting to synchronize the singing and hear Luis's message.

Attendance for the Guatemala City campaign topped 827,000. 3,800 registered public decisions.

The longest campaign Luis and his team ever carried out, Mission to London, took place in two separate phases in 1983 and 1984. In the fall of 1983 they held nine regional crusades in and around London over the course of seven weeks. 210,000 people attended the meetings and 8,000 responded to public invitations.

In those days it was impossible to buy time to broadcast the gospel in England. However, the British Broadcasting Corporation became intrigued with what was happening. The BBC decided to produce an hour-long documentary on the crusades, focusing on the gospel message Luis was preaching. The documentary aired on New Year's Day 1984 and was viewed on television by millions of people. From testimonies received afterwards, it appears that many individuals were led to saving faith in Christ through that broadcast.

The following spring Luis, then forty-nine years of age, returned to London for a six-week crusade in Queen's Park Rangers Stadium. The local committee working with Luis's team was very nervous about the large amount of money it was going to cost.

The committee asked Luis to visit Sir Morris Laing, the son of a well-known Christian philanthropist.[2]

---

2 A wealthy person who makes generous financial donations to worthy causes.

The committee hoped Luis would be able to gain Sir Morris's verbal and financial support of the crusade. His example would encourage others to do the same.

Luis arrived for his private appointment with Sir Morris right on time. Morris greeted Luis abruptly with just two words: 'Morning. Tea?'

'Yes, please,' Luis replied.

Morris poured tea for both of them, and they sat down. 'I have fifteen minutes for you,' he informed Luis. 'I must go to the city to meet with the head of Royal Dutch Shell and another business partner.' He sipped his tea, then looked Luis straight in the eye and asked directly, 'What do you want from me?'

'Well, sir,' Luis began, 'I don't want anything from you. But the executive committee for our London evangelistic campaign informed me that they are under extreme financial pressure. They say that God has given you contacts and resources that may help us. They also told me that you have a heart for the city and the nation.'

'I know what they want,' Morris stated. He got up and went to his desk. Returning to Luis, he handed him a check and asked, 'Will this do?'

Luis was amazed to see that the check was made out for 100,000 pounds! Back then that was an 'astronomical' amount of money. 'I think it will encourage the committee,' Luis responded in understated fashion and with a chuckle.

'Good,' replied Morris. He then revealed: 'I've been asking around carefully about you. I don't want to get involved in anything that might give my business a bad name. But you seem honorable.'

He added: 'There is another check for that same amount if you come up short at the end. Please tell no one, because I do not like to give alone. Let's get others involved.'

Luis had lunch with the campaign committee early that same afternoon. When he pulled Sir Morris's check out of his pocket, they all gasped. The committee chairman then removed an envelope from his jacket.

'This is of the Lord,' he stated earnestly of the enormous donation. 'I had a letter of resignation in my pocket. If he had not given this, I couldn't have carried on. I wouldn't have had the courage.'

Sir Morris's support of the campaign opened doors to the highest levels of British society. Dozens of events were held to further prepare for the large stadium meetings. They even held a prayer breakfast for members of Parliament at the Speaker's house. Newspapers, magazines, television, and radio contributed to the swell of interest in the campaign.

318,000 individuals attended the 1984 London crusade meetings, with 20,000 making public decisions. Among those committing their lives to Christ were a rock star, a famous actress, a professional soccer player, successful businesspeople, a disillusioned policeman, at least one BBC staff member, the official crusade photographer, a man whose wife had prayed for his salvation for twenty-one years, and not a few religious ministers. Young people who professed faith in Jesus included twenty-five boys at a British boarding school, a runaway teenager, and a gang member who had helped disrupt the meeting earlier that same evening.

Another young person who became a Christian during the crusade was a ten-year-old boy named Matt Redman. Matt's father committed suicide when he was only seven years of age, leaving behind a confused son with unanswered painful questions like, 'Was his death due to anything about me?' and 'Did he not love us enough to stay around?' Things grew worse when Matt's mother remarried an abusive man.

Although Matt knew about God, he had never had a personal relationship with Him. Then the boy heard Luis preach at QPR Stadium that God is the perfect Father, in contrast to human fathers with their faults and failings. His young heart was touched, and he placed his trust in Jesus as His Savior. Matt went on to become a famous Christian songwriter and wrote such well-known songs as 'Blessed Be Your Name,' 'You Never Let Go,' and 'The Heart of Worship.'

Another convert during the 1984 Mission to London was a man who until recently had been an alcoholic. Just three weeks earlier he nearly died and was rushed to a local hospital. Afterward he attended a crusade meeting at the stadium and responded to the public invitation. His life was dramatically changed, he was completely freed from alcohol, and he even began singing in the crusade choir.

After one meeting a lady led a group of six individuals up to Luis and shared, 'I was converted at last year's crusade.' Her eyes sparkled as she added: 'And since then all six of these people have received Christ into their hearts – my husband, his sister, my two daughters, my fourteen-year-old son, and my best friend. May we have our picture taken with you?'

To top it all off, during the final week of June Luis's messages were broadcast to the entire British Commonwealth, made up of over fifty nations. About all these blessings and fruitful results in England, Luis emphatically stated, 'To God alone be all the glory!'

The London crusade committee and many churches took seriously their responsibility to care for the new believers who came to Christ during the campaign. An in-depth follow-up survey conducted six months after the campaign revealed that nearly 80 percent of all adult decision makers were active in local churches.

During the fall of that year, 1984, Luis held a pair of crusades in two of Peru's largest cities. At that time communist guerrilla fighters were trying to push the nation into lawlessness and revolution. In an effort to create a new society, they had wiped out whole villages, executing military and civil authorities, as well as martyring Christian leaders. They had killed more than forty pastors and 400 other Christians. They also invaded the United Press International offices in the capital of

Lima, blew up an American owned department store, and attacked the American Embassy.

Luis and his team realized the terrorists might launch a violent attack as the evangelist sought to share the Christian gospel. But they determined to carry out the meetings despite the danger.

They rejoiced when the weeklong crusade in the city of Arequipa was completed without trouble. Nearly 6,000 made public commitments to Christ.

After the final meeting in Arequipa, however, the night before Luis was to fly to Lima for the next crusade, the guerillas sent a messenger with a written warning: Luis must get out of Peru immediately or die 'a painful dog's death.' Luis was not sure exactly what that meant, nor was he anxious to find out!

The first six days of the Lima crusade meetings proceeded smoothly. But on the seventh night a series of explosions were suddenly heard. The terrorists were seeking to blow up the city's electrical power plants.

The crowd gasped when the stadium lights flickered. Luis realized that if power was lost in the stadium, hundreds of people could be severely hurt or lose their lives in the panic and chaos that would follow.

Nearly the entire city lost its power and was plunged into darkness. However, Alianza Stadium and the neighborhood surrounding it remained fully lit.

Luis took a deep breath, then continued preaching with even greater urgency. He desired thousands more to trust Christ before it was too late.

The last two nights of the crusade were rescheduled as afternoon meetings. 40,000 people packed into the stadium for the campaign's final meeting, and 3,000 people publicly committed their lives to Christ. Altogether, 240,750 individuals attended the Lima meetings, and 15,640 public decisions were recorded.

Luis's evangelism team continued to make as much use of radio and television broadcasting as possible to help spread the good news of salvation. During Easter Week of 1985 they blanketed the Spanish-speaking world with Luis's evangelistic messages on more than 330 radio and 480 television stations.

The following Easter of 1986 Luis kicked off a twenty-five day campaign in his homeland of Argentina with a huge opening rally of some 80,000 people in Buenos Aires. A total of 333,000 individuals attended crusade meetings in six cities throughout the campaign, with more than 12,300 responding to public invitations.

In addition, an estimated total audience of eighteen million viewers watched the six live evangelistic call-in television broadcasts that Luis hosted during the campaign. Luis and his team were astounded when hundreds of viewers kept calling in for hours after the program went off the air each night. Trained biblical counselors were still leading callers to Christ all day long and halfway through the night a week after the evangelistic broadcasts had ended.

First Ministries in Asia, Africa and Eastern Europe

Later that spring of 1986, Luis held his first-ever campaign in Asia. It took place in Singapore, an island country in southeast Asia. During the weeklong crusade, 337,500 people attended the meetings at Singapore's National Stadium, and 11,900 publicly committed their lives to the Lord Jesus.

The Far East Broadcasting Company, Trans World Radio, HCJB, and many other missionary radio and television ministries partnered together in broadcasting five of Luis's Singapore crusade messages. Those messages were simultaneously translated into eight major Asian languages and broadcast across the continent of Asia via a radio and video network.

Hundreds of thousands of copies of an evangelistic booklet that Luis had written entitled *What Is a Real Christian?* were published as well. This went on to become the most popular booklet Luis ever wrote, with more than ten million copies being distributed around the world.

Thousands were won to Christ through this multi-faceted outreach effort, which was called Asia '86. Some of those led to saving faith in Jesus were in the communistic People's Republic of China. As a result of this initial Singapore campaign, invitations began pouring in for Luis to hold crusades in Hong Kong, India, Indonesia, Japan, the Philippines, Thailand, and other Asian countries.

In March of 1987, Luis carried out campaigns on the South Pacific island nations of Fiji and New Zealand. Those crusade meetings were attended by 318,600 people, with 11,430 public decisions being made.

That same spring Luis had his first opportunity to preach the gospel in Africa. 6,000 people attended his one-night evangelistic rally in Nairobi, Kenya. 350 individuals responded publicly to the salvation invitation that evening.

That summer Luis ministered for the first time in Eastern Europe, all of which was under communism at that time. For eight days he held large tent meetings in Dziegielow, Poland, near a heavily populated industrial area along the country's southern border. 27,600 attended the meetings, and 564 registered public commitments to Christ.

'I believe we're on the verge of seeing God do great things in Eastern Europe,' Luis stated publicly during those meetings. He was thinking of seeing thousands come to faith in Christ. He had no way of knowing that communism would soon collapse in Europe, and within four years his team would see more than 101,000 Eastern Europeans commit their lives to the Lord Jesus.

Later in 1987 Luis and his team conducted an eight-day campaign in Hong Kong. 219,100 people attended the meetings, including a number from the People's Republic of China. A communist college professor came one night and placed his trust in Jesus as his Savior.

Another evening a hush fell over the stadium as Luis invited everyone to turn their eyes upward to the stars and to think about who made them. At the close of that service thousands of people flooded the field to commit themselves to Christ. In all, more than 31,260 individuals made public decisions during that campaign. That was by far the largest number of people (and the highest percentage of attendees) to make public commitments in any of Luis's crusades up to that point.

Although Luis had held campaigns in many South American countries, he had never done so in Brazil, the continent's largest nation. In 1988 he conducted four days of meetings in Porto Alegre, Brazil, which were attended by 37,000 individuals.

Portuguese rather than Spanish is the primary language spoken in Brazil. While Portuguese closely resembles Spanish, many similar-sounding words in the two languages have slightly different meanings. For that reason Luis chose to preach in English rather than in Spanish in Brazil. He was blessed to have a godly, talented interpreter who effectively translated his messages into Portuguese.

For seven nights Luis's live call-in television counseling program was broadcast during prime time in Porto Alegre. The name of the city means 'Port of Happiness.' It was far from that, as many Brazilian women and children had been abused and abandoned there.

One such woman who had been deserted by her husband, and who was now living in sin in an effort to support her three children, phoned the counseling program for help. She gained forgiveness for her sins and freedom from her guilt by trusting in Jesus as her Savior. The crusade team immediately put her in touch with a local church near her home. The church lovingly cared for the woman and her children, ministering to them spiritually and providing practical assistance with their material needs.

For many years Luis had desired to go to India to preach the gospel to Hindus. He had his first opportunity to do so in November 1988, when his team had a 'Festival of Joy and Hope' in the city of Cuttack in eastern India.

There were 3,000 Hindu temples in that area, but only about 3,000 Christians in Cuttack. Severe anti-conversion laws strongly discouraged people from leaving the Hindu faith to become Christians. But during Luis's five-day campaign, 41,000 people attended the crusade meetings, and over 4,100 publicly committed their lives to Christ.

Campaign volunteers visited 100,000 homes in Cuttack, distributing Scripture portions and inviting people to the evangelistic meetings. One visitation team was attacked and beaten by a group of extremists, but then released. As a result, more than 100 policemen were on duty at every crusade meeting. They heard the gospel clearly presented, and several placed their faith in Jesus, including one high-ranking officer.

In mid-August of 1989 a six-day crusade took place in Bogota, Colombia. The drug cartel there had just declared 'total and absolute war' on the nation. The country's leading presidential candidate was assassinated. Other killings, machine-gun fire, dynamite blasts, and arson were reported in the news that week. Despite the dangers and chaos, 166,000 people attended the crusade meetings, and nearly 10,300 individuals responded to the public invitations.

By God's grace, a disaster was avoided on the final night of the campaign. That day the police discovered arson equipment had been smuggled into where the crusade was being held. With 23,000 people jammed into the stadium and more than 6,000 more crowded outside, the stadium gates were locked during the crusade service. If the firebomb had not been discovered by the police, a horrific catastrophe would have taken place, with people trapped inside the burning stadium.

A few weeks later Luis had the opportunity to minister for the first time in the Union of Soviet Socialist Republics (U.S.S.R.), more commonly called the Soviet Union. For ten days he preached in five large cities located in four republics. One of those cities was

Moscow, capital of the Soviet Union. 40,000 people attended the crusade meetings in Olympic stadiums and other prominent settings.

The Soviet people came under heavy conviction of their sin as they listened to God's Word being preached. 'People want to confess their sins to God,' Luis's Russian translator informed him. 'When you lead them in prayer, say, "God, forgive my sins. God, forgive my sins."'

Sometimes Luis led the people in repeating that phrase three times, and their volume increased noticeably each time they repeated it. During each meeting there were moments when people would suddenly start weeping or shaking as they came under conviction from the Spirit of God. Remarkably, a total of 8,500 individuals, more than one out of every five in attendance, made public decisions during the campaign.

For many years Communist Soviet officials had suppressed Christianity and persecuted Christians. Now, in addition to allowing Luis to publicly preach the gospel, high-level officials even gave permission to use the government's own presses to print one million evangelistic booklets. Those booklets were distributed in all fifteen Soviet republics.

That November communism suddenly collapsed in the U.S.S.R. Within two years the Soviet Union dissolved into a number of independent nations.

Luis's evangelistic association often spent two or three years making all the necessary preparations for its major campaigns. However, early in 1990, top Christian leaders from Romania pleaded with the evangelist to hold a crusade in their country. 'With the collapse of dictatorship,' the church leaders explained, 'a void has been created – in politics, in economics, and especially in the spiritual realm. It is extremely important that you bring the good news of salvation through Jesus Christ to our people.'

Luis arrived in Romania just two days after the nation's first free elections in more than fifty years. 'You Romanians are now politically free,' he told each audience to which he preached, 'but you can also be spiritually free.'

Over nine days he proclaimed the gospel to 215,000 people in three cities. Incredibly, 46,170 people – again more than 20 percent of all attendees – made public decisions during that campaign.

Early the following year, 1991, Luis led the Christians of Costa Rica in celebrating a century of gospel proclamation in their country. More than 233,000 people flocked to the short four-day crusade.

That spring Luis returned to Romania for an eleven-day campaign in five cities. 125,900 people attended the meetings, and an astounding 39,445 public decisions were recorded. That is, more than 30 percent of the individuals in attendance made public commitments to Jesus.

The last crusade meeting of that five-city campaign was held in Constanta. When Luis gave the salvation invitation that night, it at first looked like everyone had left his or her seat and come forward.

'Have they misunderstood?' Luis wondered to himself. So he clarified to the throng of people who had gathered in front of the crusade platform: 'If you've just invited Jesus Christ to come into your life, if you've just accepted God's forgiveness of your sins, raise your hand.'

Nearly everyone lifted a hand! That evening 8,200 people – four out of every five people in the audience – had come forward indicating they were placing their trust in Christ as their Savior!

'Is this more than you expected?' a journalist asked the crusade chairman.

'Sure!' the chairman responded with a huge smile on his face. 'We are just 1,500 evangelicals in Constanta, a town of half a million people. We have only four evangelical [gospel-preaching] churches. What a wonderful and blessed time this has been. After forty-five years of communism, it's incredible to see such a deep desire in the heart of so many people to receive Christ.' (1,500 Christians in a city of half a million equaled only three believers for every thousand people.)

Luis's team and the Romanian Christians were amazed at the remarkable work of God in drawing over 85,600 individuals to Jesus as Savior and Lord in one year's time. In addition, more than 1,000 new churches were planted.

Increased Ministry in America

Even as Luis saw more and more doors opening to preach the gospel throughout the world and watched as God drew large numbers of people to faith in Christ, he became increasingly burdened about the spiritual needs of his adopted country, the United States of America. According to Gallup, a prominent polling agency, nine out of ten Americans at that time believed in God, and a large majority even claimed to be Christians. At the same time, however, America was obviously and quickly becoming increasingly secular (non-religious). Rapidly growing numbers of Americans no longer professed to have or live by religious beliefs.

Each year from 1970 to 1977, Luis had held smaller, shorter evangelistic rallies (rather than larger, longer campaigns) in the United States. All together those modest U.S. rallies were attended by 48,500 people, or an average of 6,062 each year. Total public spiritual decisions registered at those rallies averaged only around 100 per year.

Luis's first large-scale evangelistic campaign in the U.S. was the Spanish-language crusade he conducted in Los Angeles in 1980, not long after his wife's cancer surgery. Throughout the remainder of the 1980s Luis and his associates carried out at least one longer campaign each year (except 1988) in the United States. Several of those years (including 1988) they also held shorter rallies in U.S. cities.

Luis longed to see the gospel presented more widely in America and larger numbers of Americans turning to Christ, as was happening in other parts of the world. While continuing his evangelistic ministries to other countries, he believed the time had come for him to increase his outreach efforts in America.

Early in 1989 Luis received an unexpected phone call from Billy Graham. The famous evangelist was calling to encourage Luis in his evangelistic ministries. 'Luis, I just saw that article in *Christianity Today* magazine,' Dr. Graham began, 'about your recent crusades in various countries. Goodness gracious, you're all over the world these days!'

After they had talked for several minutes about the great work God was doing in various parts of the world, Luis took a deep breath and said: 'Billy, I've got to ask your blessing on something.' Luis explained the growing concern he had come to have about the spiritual needs of America. Continuing on, he stated: 'I believe the time has come that I should accept more crusade invitations in the States and really go for the bigger cities. But I want to feel that I have your full blessing.'

'Well, you don't need my blessing,' Mr. Graham responded. 'But if you want it, you've got it. Get on with it! Everybody talks about evangelizing America. Now let's really do it.'

Not long after that, the board of directors of Luis's ministry organization voted to start accepting invitations for evangelistic campaigns in as many as four large American cities each year. Meanwhile, Luis and his team were kept busy carrying out crusades that had already been planned in other countries. In addition, new campaign invitations continued pouring in from all over the world.

In the spring of 1991, around the same time as Luis's second campaign in Romania, he had several opportunities to speak to Christian audiences in America. 'We need a reaffirmation of Christianity's historic belief in the power of Jesus Christ alone to change lives,' he challenged those American believers.

'We've got to believe in sudden conversions again,' Luis continued. 'In the U.S. and Western Europe, we're not sure if Christ has the power to convert people suddenly. That's why we're not seeing as many conversions to Christ. If you present an anemic [powerless] Christ, who needs a three-year treatment program to get you off whatever you're on, that's the kind of Christ people are going to believe in.

'But when we proclaim, "Christ can change you now; Jesus can set you free," people will respond expecting Him to do just that. That is the power of the living Christ. That is His salvation, and it needs to be known in America.'

Later in 1991 Luis conducted a fruitful campaign in San Antonio, Texas, with 55,600 people attending and 3,070 public commitments to Christ. The following year Luis and his team carried out their largest U.S. campaign to date in Phoenix, Arizona, with 72,000 attendees and 2,346 public decisions.

For more than twenty-five years, ever since 1964, Luis had had two daily radio programs that were heard by millions of Spanish-speaking people. One program evangelized non-Christians and the other built up Christians in their faith. In 1991 and 1993 Luis launched a pair of corresponding daily radio programs in English that served those same two purposes of evangelizing unbelievers and edifying believers.

Starting in 1992 and continuing for more than a decade, a series of large Promise Keepers men's rallies were held in stadiums and arenas around the U.S. Those rallies served a twofold purpose of sharing the gospel with men who needed Jesus as their Savior and motivating Christian men to actively live out their faith.

Luis was the featured evangelist at the first Promise Keepers rally in Boulder, Colorado, in June 1992. Over the course of eleven years, he shared the salvation message at thirteen PK rallies in such cities as Detroit, Washington, Chicago, New York, Philadelphia, Los Angeles, and Cleveland. More than 357,750 men attended those thirteen rallies, with over 17,860 of them publicly committing their lives to Christ.

Beginning in 1992, about half of Luis's evangelistic endeavors during most years were carried out in the United States. In addition to those already mentioned, some of his most notable American campaigns during the 1990s included:

Grand Rapids and Holland, Michigan (1994) – 68,089 attendees, 3,662 decisions

Miami, Florida (1995) – 78,904 attendees, 3,269 decisions

Greater Chicago (1996) – 129,615 attendees, 10,112 decisions

Mission Maine (1999) – 77,615 attendees, 4,236 decisions

Luis's 'Say Yes Chicago' campaign in 1996 was his team's largest and most ambitious undertaking in the U.S. up to that point. They used a new strategy for that crusade. Rather than preaching at one primary location, they divided the greater Chicago area into nine sectors where they held significant evangelistic events. They also used a group of evangelists to preach the gospel.

During the campaign, which lasted fifty-seven days, Luis preached at twenty-seven evening meetings, including seventeen in the city of Chicago. Many of his twenty-seven messages were broadcast as live television programs in Chicago and aired nationwide on cable networks.

In all, sixty-one-year-old Luis spoke at seventy-five meetings throughout the campaign. Fifty-five specialty events were held as part of the crusade, including businessmen's breakfasts, women's luncheons, youth nights, and a concert by the popular contemporary Christian band, the Newsboys. A total of nearly 130,000 people attended the various crusade meetings, with more than 10,000 of those making public commitments to Christ.

Several other evangelists helped to proclaim the gospel during the many meetings of the Chicago campaign. Partly as a result of that shared evangelistic experience, Luis and his team founded the Next Generation Alliance (NGA) in 1998. The NGA provided training, service opportunities, and other resources for a growing number of evangelists. Within a few short years, several hundred evangelists from around the world were being trained and aided by the NGA in carrying out their vital ministries.

In 1997 and 1998 Luis carried out an amazing total of seventeen evangelistic campaigns and rallies per year! Each rally or crusade was held in a different country of the world or region of the U.S.A.

Throughout the 1990s, Luis and his team continued having crusades in many countries around the globe. Besides those already considered, among the most sizeable campaigns were:

Davao City and Manila, Philippines (1991) – 256,000 attendees, 8,459 decisions

Mexico City (1992) – 142,000 attendees, 10,500 decisions

Jamaica (1993) – 245,000 attendees, 17,500 decisions

Taiwan (1993) – 118,000 attendees, 8,600 decisions

Guatemala (1994) – 386,030 attendees, 17,158 decisions

Bolivia (1995) – 184,037 attendees, 22,011 decisions

El Salvador (1996) – 149,000 attendees, 4,850 decisions

Hong Kong (1997) – 127,740 attendees, 12,350 decisions

Villahermosa, Mexico (1999) – 117,200 attendees, 4,236 decisions

In addition, in 1998 Luis held a short crusade in Cairo, Egypt, which was attended in-person by 13,800 people. Video recordings were made of his five messages during the campaign, and each was distributed the following day to 585 churches. Approximately 110,000 people watched the videos each night. In that way, an additional 555,000 individuals viewed the taped messages, and 30,900 of those publicly committed their lives to the Lord Jesus.

Given the extremely busy travel and speaking schedule that Luis was carrying out around the world during those years, it is quite remarkable that he also managed to maintain a prolific writing ministry. Over the course of the past twenty-five years, he had authored twenty-eight books and co-authored another nine volumes! In addition, he had written numerous booklets and articles.

Three of Luis's most popular books had been published during hectic recent years: *Say Yes! How to Renew Your Spiritual Passion* (1991); *God Is Relevant: Finding Strength and Peace in Today's World* (1997); *Where Is God When Bad Things Happen?* (1999).

Many of Luis's books were written to answer the questions of non-Christians and to share the good news of salvation with them. He also wrote many books to help Christians better understand the Bible and grow stronger in their spiritual life and service.

Several of his books offered biblical guidance on subjects like dating, marriage, parenting, grief, loneliness, alcoholism, and apologetics (reasons to believe Christianity). While Luis's volumes were originally written in English or Spanish, some of them had been translated into a number of other languages as well.

A Prodigal Son Returns

During the 1993 Jamaica campaign, 17,500 public decisions were recorded. One person's commitment to Christ during the crusade was doubly precious to Luis. That was when his own son, Andrew, came to place his faith in Jesus as his Savior and Lord.

Beginning in high school and continuing through his mid-twenties, Andrew had seriously wandered from the Christian faith and healthy moral standards his parents had carefully taught him while he was growing up. For years he pursued worldly pleasures and approval, living in selfishness and sin. He was involved in drug and alcohol abuse, as well as other sins.

Luis and Pat knew Andrew was struggling spiritually, although they were not aware of the full extent of his waywardness. Once Andrew became a young adult, he was making his own independent decisions in life. His dad and mom could no longer closely guide and control his choices, as they had appropriately done when he was a child.

They did not harshly condemn their grown son, so as not to drive him away from them. He knew they did not approve of his wrong choices, even without their saying so. Instead, they continued to show their love for him and to keep the lines of communication open between them and him.

Andrew took a job in Boston, Massachusetts, and moved clear across the country from his parents and brothers who all still lived near Portland, Oregon. Luis and Pat were deeply concerned about the many worldly influences and temptations their son would likely face in Boston.

They were no longer nearby to try to help Andrew, but they knew that God still was. They prayed even more diligently, asking the Lord to protect their son from evil, and to bring people into his life who would have a positive spiritual influence on him. They also asked God to graciously draw Andrew to Jesus as his Savior, knowing that he would not find his way back to the Lord on his own.

Luis continued to keep in touch with his son by writing him encouraging letters and stopping to visit him now and again when traveling to the east coast. One freezing cold day early in 1993, Luis phoned Andrew to suggest: 'We have a crusade coming up, and I thought you might want to take some vacation time off work to join us.'

That was not Andrew's idea of an enjoyable vacation, so he replied: 'No, but thanks anyway, Dad.'

'Well, that's okay,' Luis responded. 'We just thought you might be interested because this crusade is in Kingston, Jamaica.'

Andrew instantly thought of escaping the wintertime cold of Boston to spend some time on the warm, sunny beaches of Jamaica, one of the Caribbean islands. Plus he loved to fish. So he said: 'Well okay, Dad, I'll come. But only if you can set me up with a marlin fishing trip.'

The next day Luis called Andrew back to inform him: 'A friend who is helping organize the crusade has a son who is a tournament marlin fisherman. He will take you out fishing.'

While in Jamaica, Andrew was attracted by the joyful testimonies and examples of several of the island's committed Christians. Each evening he listened to his dad speak in the Kingston National Stadium. As Luis preached about the rich young ruler (of Matthew 19, Mark 10 and Luke 18) on the final night of the crusade, Andrew reflected in his heart that he wanted to be saved from his sin and to gain the gift of eternal life. He promised God that he would stop his sinful habits once and for all and break off the inappropriate relationships he was in.

Though Andrew did not go forward when his father gave a public invitation that night, he asked Jesus to be his Savior. Afterwards he told his parents and some of his new Jamaican Christian friends of the commitment he had made to Christ.

After Andrew returned to Boston, however, he fell back into his earlier sins and unspiritual friendships. Part of him wanted to change for the better, but he felt powerless to do so. He wanted to possess the security of having religion and eternal life. At the same time, he did not want to make a commitment to Jesus as the Lord (Ruler) of his life. He was unwilling to give up having a 'good time' in sin and the approval of his non-Christian friends.

At last, he honestly asked God why he could not have a close relationship with Him, as his joyous, committed Christian friends did. God answered Andrew's question by revealing his many sins of the past, as well as present transgressions that were still coming between him and the Lord. For more than three hours Andrew lay weeping on the floor, confessing his sins of which God was reminding him. He also sincerely requested and gained the deep assurance that he had received the Lord's forgiveness for any and all of those sins.

When God's heavy conviction ended, Andrew got up off the floor, feeling exhausted. At the same time, he was filled with indescribable peace and joy. His heart overflowed with thankfulness and praise to God for His willingness to free him from slavery to sin and from his burden of guilt.

Ever after that, by God's grace and with His help, Andrew faithfully followed Jesus as His Savior and Lord. Luis and Pat, too, were filled with joy and thanksgiving as they saw not only Andrew, but all four of their sons, actively living for and serving God.

Their two older sons, Kevin and Keith, had started serving with the Luis Palau Association in the mid-1980s. Kevin's leadership abilities became apparent, and in the late 1990s he began directing the day-to-day operations of the LPA. Keith, though serving more behind the scenes, faithfully and capably carried out various ministry responsibilities for the LPA.

Andrew was intensely grateful to God for dramatically rescuing him from sin and graciously granting him the gift of eternal life. He was eager and determined to share with others what God had done for him, and what He would similarly do for all who would trust in Jesus as their Savior. Others recognized and affirmed Andrew's special gift of sharing the good news of salvation. In time, he started sharing the responsibility of preaching the gospel with his father during some evangelistic meetings.

Stephen, the Palau's youngest son, became a teacher in the early 1990s, serving at the same elementary school he had attended as a boy. His primary ministries were the loving, faithful service he provided for his family and students.

New Ministry Methods

As the 1990s drew to a close, Kevin and Andrew began encouraging their father to consider making some big changes to how they carried out their evangelistic outreaches, in order to make them even more effective. While their exact conversations about these matters were not recorded, it is known that their discussions included suggestions and considerations like these:

'Times are changing, Dad,' Kevin took the lead in introducing the topic. 'People don't seem as interested as they used to be in going to a stadium to listen to a preacher. It's more difficult now than it used to be to attract large crowds to our meetings. People's lives are busier than ever. With all the other activities and distractions competing for their attention, it is harder than ever to get people to attend.'

Luis hated to admit it, but for some time, especially in the U.S., he had been noticing the very circumstances that Kevin was now clearly pointing out. So he listened as Kevin continued: 'What if we started having evangelistic "festivals"? Rather than holding crusade meetings in stadiums for several days or weeks at a time, we could have short two-day festivals in large city parks.

'Many people won't attend what they think is a serious religious service. But they would join in with what they perceive to be a fun community event. We could include enjoyable modern features that would attract people's attention and draw them to the festival.'

'What kinds of features?' Luis asked, feeling a bit skeptical.

'People love great music,' Kevin responded. 'We could feature top contemporary Christian musicians to help draw the crowds. Remember, our largest event during the "Say Yes Chicago" campaign took place at the Newsboys concert.'

'We would need to have fantastic food available,' Andrew added. 'Local food vendors and restaurants could provide that.'

'The festivals should provide something fun for the whole family,' Kevin further commented, 'to encourage parents to bring their kids. Like a Veggie Tales children's area complete with Bob and Larry. The children's area could also include face painting, a petting zoo, clowns, balloons, and other activities.'

'We could also have a skate park,' Andrew suggested, 'featuring some of the best professional skateboarders, as well as BMX and FMX riders.[1] Some of them who know the Lord could share their personal testimonies.'

'All these features would help draw people and set the stage for them to hear the gospel,' Kevin observed.

---

1 BMX riders perform impressive jumps and other stunts using motocross bicycles, while FMX riders use motocross motorcycles.

'Evangelism would still be our primary goal in all this. Rather than having just one major preaching event each day, you could proclaim the gospel two or more times daily. Other evangelists could be invited to share the good news as well.'

At first Luis was reserved toward his sons' suggestions. For more than thirty years he had seen God work powerfully through traditional crusade evangelism. Countless thousands of people had been pointed to saving faith in Jesus through simple, straightforward evangelistic meetings and messages.

Luis did not personally enjoy loud modern music, and he knew nothing about skateboarding and BMX or FMX riding. Yet he had to admit that many young people were attracted to such entertainment, and it might provide greater opportunities for him to share the good news of salvation with more individuals.

Still, he could not help but share some of his own doubts to his sons: 'I don't know, boys. Would people really attend these festivals? Even if they did, would they actually listen to the gospel? Or would they just come for the entertainment and be too distracted by it to seriously consider their need of salvation?'

'I think such festivals have the potential to be a huge success,' Kevin responded optimistically. 'In fact, I believe they could draw larger crowds and result in more people hearing the gospel than our traditional crusade meetings do.'

In the end, it was decided that the first evangelistic festival would be held in Portland, Oregon, in 1999. A week before the festival, Luis told a newspaper reporter, 'If 10,000 people come I'll be very happy. If 50,000 people come, I'll be out of my mind."

To his surprise and the delight of his team, 93,000 individuals attended the two-day festival. This attendance was second only to the fifty-seven-day Chicago crusade three years earlier. 1,226 attendees of the Portland festival made public commitments to Christ.

The following year, another two-day festival was held in Portland. It shattered the previous attendance record for a U.S. campaign by drawing 140,000 attendees. 1,250 individuals publicly committed their lives to Jesus. Because music played such a prominent role in the first two Portland festivals, they became known as the 'Great music! Good News' festivals.

In the years that followed, Luis and his team went on to hold many evangelistic festivals in other U.S. cities. Overall, those festivals saw higher attendances and more public decisions than Luis's former U.S. crusades. Among the highest attended American festivals were:

Puget Sound Region (2002) – 151,700 attendees, 4,021 decisions

Fort Lauderdale, Florida (2003) – 340,375 attendees, 7,968 decisions

Minneapolis, Minnesota (2004) – 200,000 attendees, 9,819 decisions

Houston, Texas (2006) – 225,000 attendees, 3,875 decisions

Portland, Oregon (2008) – 185,000 attendees, 2,316 decisions

Luis was thrilled to have Andrew join him as one of the primary evangelists at some of those festivals.

The 2003 'Beachfest' in Fort Lauderdale proved to be the largest evangelistic event Luis and his team ever held in America. The festival was aimed at reaching college students during their spring break.

Each spring hundreds of thousands of students flock to Florida looking for fun on the sunny beaches. Sadly, many also seek happiness through alcohol and immoral parties. However, some of those same students are searching for deeper meaning and purpose in life. Luis and his associates were able to help nearly 8,000 individuals find answers to life's deeper spiritual needs by leading them to Jesus as their Savior.

While the main festival was held in Fort Lauderdale, it was broadcast live on more than 1,200 radio stations. Beachfest was also linked via satellite to more than twenty mini festivals held simultaneously in major cities across America.

The 2008 Portland 'CityFest' introduced a strategic new form of service evangelism called 'Season of Service.' 625 churches along with civic and business leaders throughout the larger Portland region joined together in helping to address pressing physical and material needs of the poor and hungry, homeless people, individuals without medical insurance, and public schools. 22,000 volunteers took part in the special Season of Service which lasted from May to September. Season of Service later became a regular feature of all Luis Palau festivals.

Two-day evangelistic festivals were highly effective in other countries as well. They were especially popular in Latin American countries where people love fiestas. Several of the festivals bore much spiritual fruit:

Buenos Aires, Argentina (2003) – 851,942 attendees, 28,152 decisions

Mar del Plata, Argentina (2004) – 311,300 attendees, 9,800 decisions

Lima, Peru (2004) – 667,000 attendees, 42,200 decisions

Costa Rica (2006) – 410,000 attendees, 17,405 decisions

Monterrey, Mexico (2007) – 401,950 attendees, 15,741 decisions

Buenos Aires, Argentina (2008) – 850,000 attendees, 19,463 decisions

Jamaica (2008) – 350,800 attendees, 21,207 decisions

Luis's 2003 festival in Buenos Aires turned out to be the largest campaign of his entire career, with attendance nearing 852,000. The 2004 festival in Lima saw the

second highest number of public decisions – 42,200!
– ever made in a Luis Palau campaign.

In 2000 Luis visited the People's Republic of
China for the first time and was able to preach in
three churches. He returned for his first evangelistic
campaign in China in 2004. The crusade was held in
Beijing, China's capital city. Not surprisingly, given the
strict and intimidating control the Chinese Communist
Government exercised over its citizens, the number of
attendees and public decisions were relatively small.
Still, 9,663 people attended, and 322 brave individuals
made public commitments to Christ.

While in China, Luis met a government official
named Zhao Qizheng, who was the Minister of
Information for the People's Republic of China. Luis
befriended Minister Qizheng, who was an atheist. Luis
discussed Christianity and atheism with him, seeking
to lead him to faith in Christ. A few years later they
wrote a bestselling book together entitled *A Friendly
Dialogue Between an Atheist and a Christian*.

'Burning on for God'

When Luis was sixty years old, he had stated: 'While I don't believe in "burning out for God", I do believe in burning on for Him with all my heart, soul, and strength.' By 2009 Luis was in his mid-seventies and still burning on brightly in his service for the Lord, with all the spiritual, mental and physical energy he possessed.

In the years that followed, Luis and his team continued to carry out campaigns in North and South America, the Caribbean, Europe, Africa, Asia, and the South Pacific. In 2011 Luis conducted an evangelistic festival in Ho Chi Minh City (also called Saigon), the largest city in Vietnam. That festival helped celebrate the one hundredth anniversary of the establishment of the Protestant Church in Vietnam.

While Luis remained active in his worldwide evangelistic ministries, his sons Andrew and Kevin came to have increasingly prominent leadership roles in the Luis Palau Association. Next to his father, Andrew became the LPA's leading evangelist and headed up many of its evangelistic campaigns. In 2010 Kevin became the President and Chief Executive Officer of the LPA.

Beginning in 2012 Luis and his associates began making plans for an enormous campaign in New York City during the summer of 2015. Ever since Luis was a young man in Argentina more than fifty years earlier, he had been fascinated with New York City and had dreamed of reaching it with the gospel someday.

By now Luis had been heard on the radio in New York for some thirty years, preaching the gospel in both Spanish and English. His name and preaching were well-known there. The goal of Luis and his team was to saturate New York City and the tristate area[1] with the good news of salvation.

For a full year leading up to the summer of 2015, thousands of volunteers from local churches carried out much-needed community service projects across the city. That service campaign was called NY CityServe. It culminated in a three-and-a-half-month evangelistic campaign called CityFest throughout that summer.

Luis's team partnered with more than 1,700 local churches to hold 120 evangelistic outreaches around the city. Some of those events took place at such well-known locations as Central Park, Times Square, and Radio City Music Hall. Other outreaches included neighborhood events, luncheons for businesspeople, and a gathering at the United Nations. The evangelistic efforts were featured on television and radio, as well as in newspaper interviews.

---

1 Parts of New York, New Jersey and Connecticut

New York City is a melting pot of many different nationalities. 220 languages are spoken there. This diversity was reflected in the churches that supported the New York campaign. Churches representing many different denominations and ethnic groups participated, including Latinos, African Americans, Chinese, Korean, Whites, and others.

'How do you manage to unite all these people and all these cultures?' one New York Times reporter asked.

'Jesus,' Luis replied. 'Believe me, it's because of Jesus.'

Luis was then eighty years old, and still active as an evangelist. He and his son Andrew shared the evangelistic preaching in the campaign. Luis and Andrew invited people to come to faith in Christ each time they spoke during the campaign.

Luis thought they would have been able to attract half a million people to a rally in Central Park. But following the September 11, 2001, terrorist attack on the Twin Towers, which resulted in the deaths of over 2,750 people, city officials had severely limited the numbers of people who could come together in various public places. As a result, 60,000 individuals, the maximum number allowed, gathered in Central Park to hear the gospel proclaimed. The event was recorded on video for broadcasting across the U.S. and beyond.

When Luis's organization asked permission to hold an evangelistic event in Times Square, area officials flatly refused the request. The reason given was a local ordinance (law) stating that groups could not have any sound of significant volume in the square after 7:00 p.m., because of the many Broadway shows nearby. In addition, groups were only permitted to have a one-foot-high platform.

'We need a big platform and big sound,' one of Luis's representatives explained. 'We have big music, Palau speaking, and his son speaking.'

'No way,' the authorities responded.

Another of Luis's team members, an Italian from Argentina named Carlos, pushed back a bit: 'Who set up this rule? I'd like to see the rule, because this doesn't sound reasonable. This is a place for all Americans.'

When the officials went looking for the regulation, they discovered there was no such city ordinance in writing. 'Well, you still can't do it,' they told Carlos.

''Who's in charge of this?' he pressed further. 'Who makes the decisions?'

Eventually Carlos was given the name of a man whom Luis later colorfully described as 'a typical New Yorker, let's call him Frankie.' 'If you find him,' Carlos was informed, 'he probably can work something out.'

Carlos found Frankie, who redirected him to his uncle. 'Of course you can have a big platform,' the uncle responded. 'How big do you want it and where?'

'Well, here, but they say it's not possible ...'

'Don't worry. If you let us take care of the sound and the lights, we'll get you the platform.'

Luis's team wanted to project the Times Square rally on one of the large screens around the square. However, when they approached the owner of the screen which they most wanted to use, he cursed and said, 'I'm not about to rent my screen to no Protestants.'

That angered Frankie, who responded: 'He won't rent you one? I'll get you eight for the price of one.'

As a result of these developments, Luis and his team ended up with a huge platform in the middle of Times Square, from which music, testimonies, and gospel preaching were shared. All this was projected on eight large screens all around the square. Each of the eight screens was actually better than the initial screen they had unsuccessfully tried to rent.

The square was jammed with people. For three hours the good news of salvation was proclaimed. Fifteen minutes of music were alternated with fifteen minutes of verbally sharing the gospel. In that way many different groups of people heard the message as they milled about the square and stopped to listen for a time.

A Wall Street banking executive who stopped to hear the music came to faith in Christ. Unknown numbers of others received Jesus as their Savior on that occasion as well.

Afterwards, the chairman of the New York campaign stated: 'Never in my wildest visions did I think I'd hear heaven and hell openly preached about in Times Square.'

As a result of the entire, extended New York campaign, untold thousands of people committed their lives to Christ. The Luis Palau Association estimated that up to 80 percent of New Yorkers had a chance to hear the gospel because of the team's evangelistic endeavors shared across radio, television, print media, and in other ways. At that time New York City had a total population approaching eight and a half million people.

Finishing the Race

Remarkably, Luis was enabled by God to carry out evangelistic campaign ministry clear into his early eighties. When the number of campaigns he was involved in began to decline, he continued to minister actively at conferences and churches.

Near the end of 2017, at age eighty-three, Luis returned from a period of ministry in Britain with what he thought was a chest cold. But a medical examination revealed that he had cancer in one lung. Early the next year, after further tests were run, Luis and his family were shocked to learn he had stage four lung cancer.

The cancer had already spread to his lymph nodes and other parts of his body. It was considered incurable. Unless God miraculously healed him, he might have only weeks or months to live.

When Luis first received this news, he wept. He was not afraid of dying or what would happen to him after he died. For several decades he had preached the Bible's truths that, after dying, Christians immediately go to heaven. There they spend all eternity with the Lord, enjoying Him and His countless wonderful blessings.

Luis knew all this was what he had to look forward to. Still, he wept because he could not bear the thought of being separated for a time from his wife and sons whom he loved and cherished so dearly.

Luis passed through a few discouraging weeks coming to grips with the fact that his earthly life would likely come to an end soon. During those weeks he spent much time in prayer and Bible study, seeking God's guidance in what he was facing. Through that period of soul-searching, Luis's discouragement lifted. He came to have settled peace and joy about going to be with the Lord in heaven.

Many people let Luis know they were praying for his healing. He knew God could and would heal him if that were the Lord's will. However, he sensed God was, instead, preparing him for death and going to live with Him in heaven.

Some of the Scripture verses God used to encourage Luis included:

'So do not fear, for I am with you; do not be dismayed, for I am your God. I will strengthen you and help you; I will uphold you with my righteous right hand' (Isaiah 41:10).

'Even though I walk through the valley of the shadow of death, I will fear no evil, for You are with me; Your rod and Your staff, they comfort me' (Psalm 23:4).

'For I am already being poured out like a drink offering, and the time has come for my departure. I have fought the good fight, I have finished the race, I have kept the faith. Now there is in store for me the crown of righteousness, which the Lord, the righteous Judge, will award to me on that day' (2 Timothy 4:6-8a).

'Therefore He [Jesus Christ] is able to save completely those who come to God through Him, because He always lives to intercede for them' (Hebrews 7:25).

Letters poured in from people all around the world, who shared how the Lord had used Luis to bring special blessings to their lives, their towns, and sometimes their entire regions. Those letters encouraged Luis by reminding him that God had allowed his life and ministry to count for great and eternal good. The letters also humbled him, for he realized that God deserved all the glory for using him as He did, despite Luis's limitations and shortcomings.

Luis could look back on his life without regrets over how he had used it for the Lord. Near the end of his life, he wrote:

Though I regret my many stupidities and sins, I have no regret in pouring out my years, from the time I was a boy, for the sake of the Good News. If I was given a thousand lifetimes, I would dedicate them all to the same calling. I am so glad I lived that way.

At the judgment seat, in the middle of all my stumbles, this much I know: I will be able to say to the One seated on the great white throne: 'I obeyed you, Father. You said go, and I went.'

I went. He went with me, every mile. And it was worth it.

Another great joy at the end of his life was knowing that the Luis Palau Association was being left in the capable ministry hands of his sons and the organization's other dedicated leaders. By this time the LPA had a total of nearly 100 staff members serving in its Beaverton headquarters and its other offices around the globe. Luis knew the LPA's longstanding mission of spreading the good news of salvation throughout the world would continue to be carried out by the next generation of faithful evangelists.

After receiving his cancer diagnosis, Luis needed to step back from most public ministry. He still periodically participated in evangelistic campaigns and other ministries as he was able.

He also wrote one final book, *Palau: A Life on Fire*. In it he reflected on his life and ministry, and shared about many of the people who had played important roles in helping him in his spiritual life and service.

Throughout his ministry career of more than sixty years, Luis proclaimed the gospel in-person to some thirty million people in over eighty countries. He carried out more than 480 evangelistic crusades, festivals and rallies.

Through Luis's live speaking events, radio and television broadcasts, books and magazine articles, CDs and DVDs, as well as online podcasts and blogs, he had reached more than one billion people! At the end of his life, his radio programs were still being broadcast on 3,500 stations in forty-eight countries, thus continuing to minister to millions.

Altogether, Luis had written more than fifty books and booklets, along with many magazine articles. Some of his volumes were translated into dozens of other languages, including Afrikaans, Chinese, Dutch, Finnish, German, Korean, Portuguese, and Swedish.

Luis lived a little over three years after receiving his cancer diagnosis. At first chemotherapy and immunotherapy treatments were blessed by God in battling the cancer.[1] Early in 2021, however, Luis's health worsened. He was hospitalized in February and decided to discontinue further medical treatment.

Luis died peacefully in his sleep at his home in Portland on March 11, 2021, surrounded by his loving family. He was eighty-six years old at the time of his going to be with his Lord and Savior in heaven.

Luis and Pat had been married nearly sixty years. Since her husband's passing, Pat has remained involved with the Luis Palau Association team.

---

1 Chemotherapy kills cancer cells while immunotherapy boosts the body's ability to fight disease.

Luis Palau: Timeline

1934	Luis Palau, Jr, is born in Ingeniero Maschwitz, Argentina, on November 27.
1942	Luis attends Quilmes Preparatory School.
1944	Shortly after Luis's tenth birthday, his father dies unexpectedly.
1946	Luis starts attending St Alban's College, near Buenos Aires.
1947	Luis believes in Jesus Christ as his Savior on February 12, while at Bible camp.
1952	Luis begins working for the Bank of London in Buenos Aires, then transfers to the bank in Cordoba.
1952-1958	Luis receives systematic Bible training and ministry experience at his church.
1959	Luis resigns his bank job to enter full-time Christian ministry, with the Overseas Crusades missionary organization.
1960	Luis begins a one-year graduate program at Multnomah School of the Bible.
1961	Luis marries Patricia (Pat) Scofield on August 5. They are approved to serve as missionaries with Overseas Crusades.
1962	Luis becomes a United States citizen. Serves as Spanish interpreter for Billy Graham during his California crusade.
1964	Luis begins missionary work in Colombia.
1966	Luis holds his first mass evangelism crusade in Bogota, Colombia.

1968	Luis becomes the Mexico field director of Overseas Crusades.
1968-1972	Luis holds many evangelistic campaigns in several South American countries.
1973	Luis's first European campaign, in Seville, Spain. He publishes his first book in English and Spanish.
1976-1978	In addition to his worldwide evangelistic ministries, Luis serves as President of Overseas Crusades.
1978	The Luis Palau Evangelistic Association is founded.
1979	Luis's first South Pacific campaign, in Newcastle, Australia.
1980	Luis's wife, Pat, is diagnosed with cancer. Luis's first large-scale campaign in the United States.
1982	827,000 attend Luis's crusade in Guatemala City, in conjunction with the centennial celebration of the Christian gospel coming to Guatemala.
1983-1984	Luis holds his two-phase Mission to London, 528,000 attendees.
1986	Luis's first Asian campaign, in Singapore.
1987	Luis's first African evangelistic rally, in Nairobi, Kenya. His first Eastern European campaign, in Dziegielow, Poland.
1989	Luis's campaign in the U.S.S.R.
1990-1991	Luis's campaigns in Romania.
1990s	Luis begins increased evangelistic efforts in the United States.
1999-2000	Luis's first two evangelistic 'festivals' are highly successful in Portland, Oregon.
2003	The largest evangelistic festival of Luis's entire career takes place in Buenos Aires.

2003	'Beachfest' in Florida, is Luis's largest U.S. campaign, with 340,375 attendees.
2004	Luis's evangelistic campaign in Beijing, China.
2008	Portland 'CityFest' introduces a strategic new form of service evangelism called 'Season of Service.'
2015	At age eighty, Luis still actively evangelizes in the New York CityFest.
2018	Luis is diagnosed with stage four incurable lung cancer.
2021	Luis dies peacefully in his sleep at his home in Portland, Oregon, on March 11, 2021, at age eighty-six.

Thinking Further Topics

A Christian Home and Church
What spiritual blessings did Luis Palau, Jr, have growing up in a Christian home? What blessings do you have?

Boyhood Schooling and Sorrow
What benefits did Luis receive through his school? How would the way in which Luis's father died help Luis cope?

Becoming a Christian
What did Luis need to do to gain eternal life? Have you received Christ Jesus as your Savior?

Trials and Temptations
What made Luis lose interest in the Lord? How did God lead Luis back to Him? Is anything leading you away from Jesus?

Learning to Trust God
How did Luis and his family need to trust God during their years in Cordoba? What lesson did Luis need to learn in his early years of evangelistic ministry?

Called to Full-time Christian Ministry
What were some of the circumstances God used to lead Luis into full-time Christian service? If God wants you to serve Him in a ministry career how might He lead you to do so?

Bible College, Marriage, and Becoming a Missionary
What important lessons did Luis learn from Major Thomas's chapel message? What can we learn from the teaching of Galatians 2:20?

Maria's Story of Tragedy and Triumph
How did God use Hebrews 10:17 to break through Maria's hard heart and lead her to trust in Jesus as her Savior? What

is also remarkable about Maria's testimony after she became a Christian?

Beginning Mass Evangelism Ministry

It required courage for the Christian young people in Bogota to take part in the public march. What are some occasions when we need courage to bear a Christian witness to others?

Reaching All Latin America for Christ

In what ways did Rosario help people materially and spiritually by being a compassionate Christian rather than a violent communist? What was amazing about the Bolivian President's request?

First Evangelistic Campaigns in Europe

How does the story of Danilo's unexpected death remind us about the importance of possessing eternal life? How do we gain eternal life with God in heaven?

Facing Atheists, Skeptics and Cancer

Bolivia's new President and the young daughter of a hotel elevator operator came to salvation through faith in Jesus. What do their stories teach us? How did Luis and Pat's faith help them through the trial of Pat's battle with cancer?

Fruitful and Dangerous Ministries

How did Sir Morris Laing use his wealth to help spread the good news? How can we do the same with our money? How did Luis show great courage in preaching the gospel in Peru despite the threats of the guerrilla fighters?

First Ministries in Asia, Africa and Eastern Europe

For decades communism had suppressed Christianity throughout Eastern Europe. What were the dramatic responses to the gospel in the U.S.S.R. and Romania when Luis was able to evangelize there?

Increased Ministry in America

Why did Luis think he needed to do more evangelistic ministry in the United States when such large percentages of people already claimed to be Christians? What does Luis's example teach us about the importance of spreading the gospel in our own country and to other nations?

A Prodigal Son Returns

How did Luis seek to help his son during the years Andrew wandered far away from the Lord? How did God graciously draw Andrew to Jesus Christ as his Savior and Lord?

New Ministry Methods

What were some of the changes Luis and his team made in switching from a 'crusade' to a 'festival' approach in evangelism campaigns? What was the one key aspect of their campaigns that they did not change?

'Burning on for God'

How does Luis's example teach us to 'burn on' for God rather than 'burning out' for Him as we go through life? How do you think the 'Season of Service' that took place before evangelistic festivals were held helped to open doors for the gospel to be heard?

Finishing the Race

In what ways did God provide Luis with assurance and peace when he learned that he was dying? How can we, like Luis, have no regrets about how we've lived for the Lord when we come to the end of life?

Christian Focus is for Kids

CF4KIDS

That means you and your friends can all find a book to help you from the CF4KIDS range – from the very littlest baby to kids that are almost too old to be called a kid anymore.

We publish books that introduce you to the real Jesus, the truth of God's Word, and what that means for boys and girls of all ages.

Reading books is a fun way to find out what it is like to be a follower of Jesus Christ.

True stories, adventures, activity books, and devotions – they are all here for you and your family.

Christian Focus is part of the family of God. We aim to glorify Jesus and help you trust and follow Him.

Christian Focus Publications Ltd,
Geanies House, Fearn, Ross-shire,
IV20 1TW, Scotland,
United Kingdom.
www.christianfocus.com